A REBEL
FROM THE
START

Setting the record straight

AVI YEMINI

About Rebel News

Rebel News is Canada's largest independent source of news, opinion and activism. Because Rebel News takes no money from any government, it is able to report candidly on controversial events, like the trucker convoy. Rebel News's motto is "telling the other side of the story" — in Canada and across the world.

For more information about Rebel News, or more copies of this book, please visit *www.RebelNews.com*

TABLE OF CONTENTS

FOREWORD
BY SYDNEY WATSON

When I think of Avi Yemini, I am reminded of Murphy's laws.

Through their cynicism, at the core of them all is one common thread: Nothing will ever go the way you think it will. For better or for worse.

This tendency of life can complicate matters. Things seldom unfold seamlessly, and this alone necessitates our constant focus to navigate the many complexities that stumble us.

This reality is both annoying and thrilling. It is the pervasive, singular force that governs the existence of all individuals, universally.

The painter Bob Ross referred to this phenomenon as "happy little accidents," a term, I confess, I really enjoy. It offers a positive lens through which to view the messy disruptions that often dominate our lives.

If there is one person who could be held up as evidence of this seemingly universal axiom, it would be Avi.

And it is precisely that which brought us together in the first place.

When we met, I was a fresh-faced 20-something who accidentally went viral on Facebook. I'd made a video about gun control that riled up Australians in a way I couldn't have foreseen. And, amidst the tidal wave of vitriol and the overwhelming anxiety of sudden notoriety, Avi was the one person who appeared on the horizon and threw me a lifeline. I'm glad I caught it.

It was also here, at this juncture, that I learned another universal life truth: yes, even the best laid plans go awry, but where there is a chaotic, headstrong Jewish man at the helm, there is a way.

No, I mean it – Avi made sure there was always a way.

Our early days muddling through the online media landscape are best described as "confusing." Actually, the entire experience felt akin to owning a puzzle with a thousand indistinguishable pieces.

Sure, we could have dumped out the box, turned the pieces over and slowly assembled the picture. But that takes time and a degree of patience that neither of us possessed.

No, instead the early days were a chaotic scene of pieces haphazardly forced together. There were no instructions, no road map, and this journey was soon punctuated with life's inherent inclination for things to often go hilariously wrong.

The truth was, neither one of us had any clue what we were doing, let alone what we had gotten ourselves into. News, writing, videos – these things are hard, even for seasoned practitioners.

It was here I learned very clearly that any undertaking involving Avi Yemini would inevitably succumb to life's general disorder.

In all honesty, it's what made working with him so immensely stressful and enjoyable. I had known many effervescent, fascinating people in my life. But none could hold court like Avi.

And, to be clear, dear reader, the puzzle pieces did eventually come together. But, as Avi describes in this book, that took some time (and a hell of a lot of patience).

For me, at the heart of our extraordinary ordinary situation, was another realization – working alongside someone unburdened by fear, when you yourself possess buckets of it, is a peculiar place to be. Avi has always possessed a fearlessness that was both inspiring and disconcerting. And I truly mean disconcerting.

No matter how often he got knocked down, he'd cackle, stand up and get knocked down all over again. Early on, I watched this with a sense of terrible foreboding. One day, this industry, his recklessness, will take him out.

He certainly fell down a few more times – but he always found a way back to his feet. I admired that. The inevitability of chaos was never a deterrent. Neither was the, at times, overwhelming deluge of criticism directed his way.

That's another thing about media: everyone's got an opinion. And everyone's prepared to tell you that yours is wrong.

According to Avi's critics, he wasn't only wrong, he was something much worse: uncredentialed. I had earned a Master of Journalism from the University of Melbourne. However underqualified I was for our field; nobody could say I didn't have a very expensive piece of paper sitting on my wall.

Avi, on the other hand, was repeatedly castigated for his lack of qualifications. As if that somehow made his work any less meaningful or important.

One of my favourite writers, Ken Follett, once essentially said that there is a societal expectation that people stay in their own lanes. Of course, he said this considerably more eloquently:

"Clowns should not try to play Hamlet. Pop stars should not write symphonies."

For Avi, it was IDF-gym owners should not become political commentators. Skeptics questioned the audacity of someone with his background daring to step a foot outside his accepted lane.

But why shouldn't he? Who is to say that an individual cannot excel in multiple arenas or break through the confines of conventional wisdom?

It is very unlikely that life will present any one of us with situations that perfectly match our strengths. We all exist in a broader societal and cultural framework that was not specifically designed or tailored to accommodate our individual capabilities.

But only a fool would let this stop him from trying. And Avi is many things, but he is no fool.

Let me put it like this, my own spin on the classic line: well-behaved Avis seldom make history.

I think we've seen that fact play out in real time.

Avi endures as one of the few people I trust implicitly. And I say this, knowing full well that he is also the responsible party who has landed me in more absurd situations than I can poke a stick at.

I once incredulously watched him from the other side of a holding area at LAX airport, while members of border security searched both our belongings.

Avi grinned and waved. I said, "I'll see you soon."

We both ended up questioned by the FBI over threats of terrorism – not that we had threatened anyone, of course. This is a great story now – but I admit the entire experience appalled me at the time.

I found out hours later Avi had been denied entry to the United States and promptly sent on a plane home to Australia.

Murphy's laws in full effect.

I should note that this same man, who inadvertently led to my encounter with the FBI, has also stuck his neck out for me countless times. It is one of his finest qualities, whether he is prepared to admit that or not.

For all our years of friendship, I learned a great deal about Avi when he allowed me to read a draft of his book.

Over the years, I have witnessed his growth and evolution, but reading his story allowed me to glimpse into the depths of his experiences and the profound lessons they have taught him.

This memoir is not the product of a tortured artist seeking catharsis or a self-indulgent politician trying to curry favor with an indifferent audience. It is the manifestation of a man with one hell of a story to tell.

Despite nature's laws of chaos, somehow, we all made it here in one piece. To write this foreword, I am honoured. And because of that, I will take this opportunity to leave you with something important:

What is remarkable is not the presence of life's inevitable problems, it is Avi's remarkable ability to overcome them.

Sydney

CHAPTER ONE

A BORN ATTENTION SEEKER

I laugh when critics accuse me of being an attention seeker. I'm the tenth of 17 children born to my mother within 20 years. I've been seeking attention my entire life just to survive.

Many media personalities claim not to care about the attention, that they're only in it for the cause, the principles, and the common good.

I call bullshit on that.

They crave attention as much as I do. They're just too scared to admit it.

Don't get me wrong, I care passionately about many of the issues I report, and I always ask myself what effect my stories have on my audience and society at large. I am an activist alright. But I still love the attention.

My quest for the limelight began the night I was born. I probably should have waited a few more days to arrive, but that's the other thing you need to know about me – I'm always in a hurry.

I made my grand entrance the night mum and dad arrived in Melbourne.

It must have been hell driving all night in a nine-seater crammed with eleven people. Mum - heavily pregnant with me - trying to entertain their nine kids while dad concentrated on the road out of Sydney.

When our tired Nissan Urvan finally came to a stop, mum probably needed a rest. But even then, I had other plans, and they wouldn't wait.

From day dot of my family's new life in Melbourne, I had to be the centre of attention. Without even the chance of settling in, I forced my parents to leave nine children at home so they could urgently get to The Royal Women's Hospital to welcome me into the world.

Being born the night we arrived in Melbourne was a family bookmarking tool used throughout my childhood.

"How long have we been here," someone would ask, immediately followed by, "How old are you, Bobom?" which is my childhood nickname.

The impulsive streak comes from my father and from his father before him. It's gotten me into a fair bit of trouble but has also served me well. Like so much of life, there are two sides to most things.

My Russian-Polish grandfather arrived in Sydney, where he met my Polish grandmother in 1937, fleeing the Nazis as they wrapped their totalitarian tentacles around Europe. Dad was a poster child for the generation that came of age in the 1960s. By his own admission, he "was totally materialistic, obsessed with sex, drugs and rock'n'roll".

But the nihilistic lifestyle eventually wore him down. He had reached a point where his entire existence felt "totally empty".

So, dad rebelled in the most dramatic way you could imagine – he found religion. And he pursued faith with the same zeal he had pursued girls.

The hard-drinking, hard-partying Stephen Waks changed his name to Zephaniah - the name of an Old Testament prophet who warned Israel of impending judgement if they did not turn from their sins - and joined an ultra-orthodox Jewish sect.

To never do things by halves was a trait my father passed down to all of his children.

But it wasn't enough for dad to join Sydney's Chabad Hasidic community. He booked a flight and headed to the group's headquarters in New York, where he found more profound theology and, more importantly, he also found my mother.

Mum's upbringing was in stark contrast to my father's. She was born to devout Yemenite Jews who fled their tiny Arab nation to live in Israel at its rebirth in 1948.

The secular youth culture that had dominated my father's early life in Sydney was utterly foreign to my mother, who was raised in Kfar Saba, a suburban town in Israel, according to strict Jewish customs.

Popular culture was - and in some ways still is - alien to her. As a girl, she never encountered boys outside her family.

"We didn't think about it, we didn't know about it, we didn't even miss it because we didn't know its existence," she would say in her typically forthright manner.

Years later, it all made sense to me after spending time in the tight-knit family neighbourhood mum grew up in. Family and religion were central to everything. A few blocks in each direction, everyone was related.

The central point of this family enclave was a courtyard with four synagogues, two of which were built by the family.

Mum's life changed forever when, at age 17, her father offered her a tantalising choice - he would pay for her to have driving lessons, or he would pay for her to leave the family enclave and fly to New York.

She chose New York.

A known Shadchan (religious matchmaker) in Crown Height's bustling Chabad community set up Zephaniah and Chaya. They went out three times over two weeks before asking the Rebbe (Chabad leader), for his blessing to get married. He immediately agreed. A month later, they were husband and wife and off to start a family in the Holy Land.

The Rebbe prophesied during their meeting that Hashem (God) would bless them with many children. My folks should have followed up with a Melbourne Cup tip because we'd later need the money.

By the time my parents decided to move from Israel to Australia in 1984, they already had eight children. A ninth was born in Sydney. And then, a year later, when they relocated to Melbourne, I arrived in a rush.

Up until grade five, one morning of every year, I'd arrive at school and announce that my mother had a baby. To which my class would respond, "mazal tov, another one?!"

Mum and dad eventually had 17 children, and they raised us with the same strictness that my mother had experienced growing up.

As kids, we did not listen to non-Jewish music, go to the movies, or read novels.

What little screen time we had was restricted to faith-orientated programming. In fact, dad had a printed sign stuck to the tv cabinet removing all doubt.

"This unit is used only for holy purposes and educational and family videos."

Occasionally, the strictness of our household, even according to Halacha (Jewish law) went too far. My mum was famous for her passionfruit ice cream, especially around Passover time. She'd make it in advance for the entire Jewish holiday week.

Needless to say, passionfruit ice cream for 17 children required a lot of passionfruit. One year my mother got tired of paying for the fruit that she reasoned she could grow herself.

I arrived home from school to see our sizeable fencing area covered in plastic trellis with a few passionfruit plants attached. It looked impressive.

Mum tended to her investment with much care, watering and mulching the plants according to the gardener's strict instructions.

However, the Torah (The Old Testament) prohibits eating the fruit of trees in their first three years. "When you enter the land and plant any tree for food, you shall regard its fruit as forbidden. Three years it shall be forbidden for you, not to be eaten." (Vayikra 19:23).

The vines grew a few meters over our fences in their first year. In the second and third years, the vines grew even bigger with an abundance of passionfruit that we 'had to' throw out. It was even forbidden to feed animals, sell, give away or use for compost.

Throwing them into the rubbish didn't quash my mother's enthusiasm for tending to the trees. "It will all be worth it next year", she said in the final year of the forbidden fruit.

Finally, the fourth year arrived, and we were all excited for what we imagined would be a year of unlimited passionfruit ice cream on Passover.

But no. The fourth year barely produced fruit.

It turned out the best years had passed. Only after that calamity did my parents learn that the prohibition of benefiting from fruit in their first three years didn't extend to passionfruit.

As if we weren't already different enough from our neighbours, we only followed the Jewish calendar.

I was about eight years old when I walked to the corner medical clinic to see a doctor about my burning tonsils. The receptionist kindly asked me what my date of birth was, and I had no idea.

The second of Cheshvan, 5746, was all I knew, but that didn't help her much. So she called my father, who had to double-check his long spreadsheet.

"Seventeenth of October, 1985", the softly spoken receptionist repeated, writing it down on the form in front of her.

That was the most secular piece of personal information I'd ever received up until that point in my life. I cherished it, engraving the date into my brain and looking forward to the next time I could use it.

At the time, dad reckoned we weren't radical. Rather, in his words, we were "on the observant side of the middle" on the spectrum of religious Jews.

Now his views have changed, but that's a whole different story.

It certainly was radical, even for the community we were a part of.

The religious outlook of my parents might have worked for them in the Middle East, but it wasn't working for me in Melbourne.

Even from a young age, though steeped in the orthodoxy of my family, I didn't want to be religious. I liked the gatherings and the parties demanded by Jewish tradition, but that was it. I didn't care for the rules and regulations.

When I wasn't being suffocated by an endless list of "thou shalt nots", I was being smothered by my numerous siblings.

Indeed, there was always someone to play with, but there was also always someone to fight with.

The enormous size of our family meant that mum and dad simply couldn't meet all the demands competing for their attention. As a kid, I quickly learnt that I would become quite literally lost in the crowd if I didn't fight for their attention.

My parents just didn't have much time for each of their kids – how would they? It wasn't an issue of there not being enough love. It was about there not being enough hours in the day. Divide 24 hours by 17 children ranging in age from toddlers to teens, subtracting time for sleep, cooking, work, chores and whatever else needed to be done, and there was not much left to go around.

The family dynamics made me who I am today. To get attention from parents or siblings, you had to be willing to do things others weren't. You had to risk embarrassment and continually put yourself out there. So, I did.

One day, when I was nine years old, I pretended to faint at school during playtime. I lay on the ground in the classroom when everyone was outside and didn't move, waiting to be found when they returned.

My heart skipped a beat when the first child noticed me lying there, "passed out". He began to call my name, checking if I was okay. I lay there motionless, doing all I could to keep up the pretence.

He screamed for help, only making it much more exciting. Within minutes I was surrounded, with all the focus on me.

As exhilarating as it was to have all the attention, I felt I was missing out as I couldn't see what was happening. So I began rolling my eyes to the back of my head, allowing me to look around, which freaked out the PE teacher, who was monitoring my pulse and breathing by this time.

"Where is the bloody ambulance, for goodness sake?!" he yelled.

Almost as if God answered him, a siren could be heard in the distance. I could feel his relief as he continued to check my vitals.

That was the first time I ever felt noticed. Two ambulances, a MICA paramedic, hundreds of students, and my teachers watched as I was wheeled away in a stretcher.

I spent the night in the hospital, where I was told that the entire school took a lesson off to pray for me in Shul (Synagogue).

It was like I had hit the attention-seeking jackpot and wasn't willing to give it up too quickly.

Over the next eighteen months, I fainted a few times a week. Avoiding school work, getting out of homework I hadn't completed, and missing tests I hadn't studied for.

After all, my "I thought Mashiach (the Messiah) would come overnight" excuse for not completing homework stopped working the first time I tried it.

Fainting was my personal saviour.

When the first Gan Yisrael (summer camp) came around, I realised I had to sacrifice the best two weeks to protect the rest of the year. I fainted two days into camp, which I had been looking forward to since the previous summer, knowing they'd send me home.

It worked. To this day most people, including my dad, believe the fainting was real. Although after months in and out of hospitals with neurosurgeons trying to figure out why I was having seizures, they realised it wasn't epilepsy as diagnosed initially.

I would hold my breath when they did scans, hoping the lack of oxygen in my brain would trick the medical machines into recording something wrong with me.

There wasn't. I really just wanted the attention.

Being in hospital wasn't convincing me to stop, either. I got to be in bed all day, avoiding school, sometimes for weeks, as nurses gave me all the love and attention I desired. Plus, being in The Children's Hospital, I was allowed to watch television for the first time. That's when I became obsessed with kids TV programs like; "Bananas in Pyjamas" and "Postman Pat".

My whole story almost came crashing down when the Paediatric Neurologist sat me in his office, alone, to tell me he knew I was faking. While, inside, I was terrified, I continued to deny it.

Walking out of Masada Hospital that day, I promised myself I wouldn't let him win. Continuing to put on this fainting act was part of my devious plan.

The specialist called us back days later, saying he had found something. I was so excited, believing holding my breath had actually worked. But after more tests, it was proven false.

None of which stopped me from fainting.

One Monday morning, when no one was watching, I passed out at school. Looking back, never collapsing in front of witnesses should have been the dead giveaway. My teacher picked me up and took me to the staff room until my father arrived. It was the only time my father questioned if I was faking. I could hear them discussing the outcome of my brain scans, which led my dad to initiate his own test. My father pinched me hard on my arm. I knew in that moment that everything was on the line. If I failed to control myself, all my hard work would be undone. It took all my mental power not to flinch, even though it hurt like hell.

With a massive bruise on my arm, I concocted a plan to ensure that would never happen again. Waiting until my parents were both in the kitchen, I showed the bruise to my mother.

"Imma, I think I fell yesterday when I fainted", I said to her, pointing at the sizeable purple mark on my upper arm.

"No, that was me, trying to see if you were awake," my father butted in.

At that moment, I knew my plan was executed flawlessly. My mother made sure I was never pinched again.

One thing I could have never controlled was if someone had tickled me. I'm not sure why no one ever tried, but laughter would have caught me out. In fact, laughing, not from tickling once, almost did give me up.

I was "unconscious" in the back of the classroom, being cared for by the teacher's aid when the other class clown cracked a joke about my fainting. I don't recall what he said, but it was funny and made me chuckle.

"Avrohom Sholom Waks, are you awake?" she asked.

"Don't move, don't move, don't move," my brain screamed at me.

Phew, it worked. She must have imagined my giggle, probably because the entire class was roaring with laughter at the time.

While I've never grown out of banter, even at my own expense, I did eventually grow out of my fainting stage through a child psychiatrist who helped me get attention in less destructive ways.

My determination to be noticed as a child has carried through to this day in my media career. I'm still the larrikin that can't control my laughter, the class clown who cracks jokes at inappropriate times, and I won't be ignored.

So, it was a complicated and chaotic house to grow up in. And I mean that both figuratively and literally.

Mum and dad bought a house in St Kilda East opposite our Jewish school and Synagogue. It was a three bedder when they arrived with nine children plus me. They later added nine bedrooms and five kitchens.

The numerous kitchens were necessary, not just because there were a lot of meals to prepare, but because strict Kosher rules meant dairy and meat products couldn't be cooked together.

Council permits for the renovations took forever because town planners were convinced mum and dad were building a brothel (It's still a mystery to me why a brothel would need five kitchens!)

As an adult, I love my large family. Even though we're so different, I'm close to all my siblings. However, as a kid, I would lie in bed at night and contemplate what it might be like to be an only child. I would dream about being adopted by a non-Jewish childless couple who could pay me attention and give me whatever I wanted.

I didn't like not having stuff. Mum and dad did their best, of course, but there wasn't any margin for nice things.

My childhood fashion was an endless series of hand-me-downs, the only way they could manage with so many siblings. All the used clothes and shoes sat in cupboards waiting to be claimed by a sibling who would fit them.

I'll never forget how jealous I was of school friends with nice stuff, especially cool shoes like Nikes.

One day I decided to change my fate. I rummaged through the hand-me-down shoe cupboard in the old part of the house to find a pair of my own. I almost cried when I succeeded.

Sure, they had seen better days. But I mean, aside from the fact that they were dirty, worn, full of holes and four sizes too big for me, they were perfect.

I wore them to school the next day.

Proudly waddling into class with a massive grin, I was pretty underwhelmed by my friends' lack of enthusiasm over my new kicks.

Whenever I was lucky enough to get new clothes, they usually came from a discount department store called Dimmeys. So, they had a particular look about them.

We would go to Dimmeys only if I needed something that couldn't be found after multiple searches of the family hand-me-down cupboards.

On birthdays we were always given an option between a present or a class party at home, and I always chose the latter, so I'd get more than 20 gifts—one from each classmate.

Although on my seventh birthday, I didn't get an option because it was also my little brother Dovi's special birthday the next day.

It's called an Upshernish, which happens on a boy's third birthday when the family invite the entire community to witness the cutting of his hair for the first time.

A decorated chair next to Dovi's was allocated for my celebration. No one seemed to notice besides me, which sucked.

Unlike today, with unlimited technological distractions, thirty years ago, kids were expected to entertain themselves outdoors. So having sixteen siblings without constant adult supervision was often fun but sometimes dangerous.

I was about seven when my 12-year-old brother invited me outside to help him build a cubbyhouse from scrap wood in the garden.

A couple of hours into construction, my mother came outside to see what we were doing.

"That doesn't look very safe," she told my brother in a concerned thick Israeli accent.

It must have looked pretty shonky because I doubt her occupational health and safety standards were exceptionally high at that point in our lives.

"Nah. Imma. This is safer than a Sukkah," my brother assured her, referring to the temporary hut constructed for use during the week-long Jewish festival of Sukkot.

"Look how strong it is," he said, lifting the roof as if to demonstrate to the compliance officer in front of him.

I don't remember how it happened, but before my mother could respond, the entire cubbyhouse collapsed, ripping my hand right open.

Many stitches later, my brother's building career was shut down.

As part of the Chabad community which I grew up in, there was a big emphasis on outreach. From as young as seven, I used to go with bar mitzvah kids on something called Mivtzoim

We would go to shopping strips, malls, businesses and residents, walking up to complete strangers and asking if they were Jewish.

Depending on the time of year, if they were Jewish, we would ask them to do a "Jewish good deed". On a typical day, we would ask a man to put on a prayer shawl and Tefillin (black leather straps tightly wrapped around their arm and head in a weird tradition that must look kinky to outsiders), or we would give a woman a card with instructions on how to light Shabbat candles. On Jewish holidays, we would ask them to perform the relevant Jewish customs for that holiday.

If they weren't Jewish, we would hand them the Seven Laws of Noah, which, according to Jews, are the only laws gentiles need to keep:

Don't worship idols.

Don't curse God.

Don't commit murder.

Don't commit adultery or sexual immorality.

Don't steal.

Don't eat flesh torn from a living animal.

Do establish courts of justice.

To be fair, I used to be jealous of their shortlist. We had 613 laws to keep, and each one had another thousand extra layers of rabbinical protection stopping you from doing anything fun in life. But that experience of being taught to walk up to strangers and strike up a conversation was excellent training for what I do now.

My upbringing wasn't all bad.

Each of us shared a room with a sibling, the older one charged with the care of the younger. When I was little, I shared with my big brother Shneur. He's eight years older than me and was given responsibility for me when his pet goat died.

We weren't allowed "non-kosher" animals, so Shneur's goat was our first and last pet.

My siblings named the animal "Honey", which probably had less to do with the goat and more to do with the fact that "honey" would have been one of the first English words our fresh-off-the-boat clan learnt due to its religious connection.

And I bet my parents were happy with the name, subconsciously trying to make Australia the new "land flowing with [goat] milk and honey".

Sadly, Honey, the goat didn't last. To this day, no-one in our family knows exactly how Honey met her demise, though I suspect the poor animal may just have been overwhelmed by the intensity of the large and ever-growing Waks family.

Shneur was devastated when the vet had to put Honey down after a few weeks of the mysterious illness. The only way mum and dad could console him was by giving him care of me.

And, fortunately for both of us, I lasted a little longer.

Until I was about 8, Shneur probably parented me more than mum and dad. Then he was shipped off to a religious boarding school, and I was put with my little brother, Didy.

Sharing a room with my little brother had its perks. Didy looked up to me for guidance that I was always keen to give, even though we were only thirteen months apart.

Didy once asked me the difference between a hardboiled egg and one that liquid came out of when it was cracked.

I had no idea. So I told Didy that he'd understand when he was older.

I was full of great wisdom like that for Didy.

School wasn't really my thing. I didn't like school. I didn't do any work at school. And I barely passed any exams at school.

However, the grade 6 graduation was a memorable evening, and I was so excited.

Moving up to year 7 was a big deal. It's the year you turn Bar Mitzvah and, according to Jewish tradition, become a real man.

The graduation ended with a presentation where each kid was asked what they wanted to do when they were older.

Most of my classmates answered, rabbi, doctor or lawyer.

I responded, farmer.

The crowd of parents and family burst into laughter.

Even though it was my honest answer and not intended for that reaction, I welcomed it.

By the time I got to high school, I was so used to getting into trouble that I wouldn't even bother going to class half the time. Instead, I'd just head straight to the principal's office—cutting out the middleman.

I may not have excelled in English and Science, but I did become super-efficient at writing lines.

I even designed a device using a ruler and four pens to write four lines simultaneously. Sure, they looked terrible, but at least I beat the system.

And once, when I actually attended a sports class in year seven, I cracked an inappropriate joke and was sent to the library to write five hundred lines. Which, even for an expert like me was an impossible amount of lines.

"You want to play that game," I thought to myself as I walked up the stairs to the library. "Let's play."

I used my four-pen device to write one page and, with ultimate chutzpah, got the librarian to help me photocopy it enough times.

Still warm from the printer, I handed my lines to the PE teacher.

To my absolute shock, he accepted them.

I gave that one class everything. Not because I was worried about being punished again. Instead, I felt I'd earned it. My participation itself became the defiant activity.

So, it wasn't exactly a surprise to anybody, least of all me, when in year Eight, I was expelled from the Orthodox Jewish School I had attended all my childhood.

CHAPTER TWO

FALLING DOWN

The only times I felt free from my authoritarian home was when I went to school or summer camps.

It was at a camp in country Victoria at age 12 that my friend and I introduced ourselves to the tzedakah box (charity box) in the camp synagogue so we could give smoking a try. Like everything in my life, I wasn't willing to do things half-assed. I went straight for the hard stuff - Marlboro Reds.

A few of us kids had designated a smoking area near a small shed out in an empty field where no one could see us.

On the final day of camp, as all the kids were boarding buses for the trip home, I snuck off to have my last cigarette before we had to leave.

After finishing it, I still had a few minutes, so I started flicking matches into the dry grass near the shed.

I'd flick a match into the grass, and then quickly stomp on the fire.

Enjoying my final minutes of freedom from strict parenting, I flicked a match into a dry bush, and oof, the whole thing lit up! My heart began to race. There was no way I was going to be able to stomp it out.

There were fields of dry grass as far as the eye could see, and I knew I was in all sorts of trouble.

I dashed into the shed and found a wheelbarrow full of what looked and smelt like manure. Without thinking, I grabbed it and rolled it straight to the bush where the grass was still burning.

With my bare hands, I grabbed poo and threw it over the fire, and then began furiously jumping on top of it.

In that thirty seconds, I made all sorts of promises to God, if he would just help me put out this fire.

God didn't appear to me in this burning bush, but he did answer my heartfelt prayers.

The fire was miraculously out.

Exhausted, I rolled the wheelbarrow back into the shed, where I noticed a fire extinguisher hanging on the wall. How I missed that, I will never know.

With my heart still pumping fast, I walked back to the car park where everyone was already boarding the bus, oblivious to the disaster that had only narrowly been averted.

As these camps didn't happen nearly often enough for my liking, I sought other ways to escape from home.

One Saturday, I planned with a friend at Synagogue that I would sneak to his house after nightfall so I could join him at an underage nightclub he frequently attended.

My friend came from a far less observant family and was allowed to participate in the world outside our closed-off community.

For me, it was going to be my very first time in a place with non-Jewish music and girls. I was so excited, I reckon I did the usual 15-minute walk to his house in under 5 minutes.

When I arrived, he was putting gel in his hair and asked if I wanted to try some. I think I answered "hell yeah" before he had even finished speaking.

AVI YEMINI

I'd recently had my Bar Mitzvah, so I was a 13-year-old who'd never gone to a professional barber. My dad would shave our heads and leave little Payot—the Jewish sideburns. So, yes, gel would save my life that night.

I hadn't had a haircut for a while because I had been growing it out since my dad's last hairdressing butchery.

A few months earlier, I was chewing gum in Rabbi Kimelman's class. Kimelman, a physically large man with a long beard, was that teacher kids knew not to mess with.

Most kids, I mean.

Rabbi Kimelman spotted my vigorous chewing and flew straight to my desk faster than I ever imagined he could move.

Reaching out his hand, "spit it here," Rabbi Kimelman demanded.

"Holy crap!" I thought to myself. "He's asking me to spit in his hand".

Refusing to miss this once-in-a-lifetime opportunity, I began loudly gathering the maximum phlegm possible before "ptooey" spitting it all in his open hand.

Before I had a chance to enjoy my classmates' reactions, Kimelman took his hand full of mucus and chewing gum, rubbing it all in my hair.

The joke was on me for now, but I couldn't wait to get home and show my parents what he had done.

However, things didn't go as planned. My dad wasn't bothered by Kimelman. In fact, he seemed excited to completely shave my head to zero, much shorter than usual, leaving only the religious sideburns.

It was a double punishment.

And took months to look relatively normal again.

But finally, here I was at my mate's place with enough length to work with. Unfortunately, I'd never used gel and ended up looking like a wannabe mafioso in my trench coat, with my greasy hair slicked back from the *Jewburns* up.

At that age, self-awareness wasn't my strong suit, so I was pretty pleased with my appearance, and off we went to the club.

It was as thrilling as I had imagined. The girls didn't let me down, and neither did the music.

When it was all over, we returned to my friend's home. I washed the gel out and stuck my Kippah (religious skullcap) back on my head, ready to go home.

I was far less excited about the stroll home. The adrenaline started kicking in, the fear of getting caught was real.

Walking up our 10-meter driveway felt like a kilometre. When I finally got to the side door, which we used as the main access to the house, my ultra-religious brother Shmaya was waiting on the other side to greet me.

I was busted. But at least it wasn't my parents.

Shamaya, seven years older than me, has always been the most fanatical about his faith in our family. So he took it especially hard that his little brother was out with girls and dancing (more like Jew-shuffling) to not-very-kosher music.

After seeing how determined I was to assimilate into Australian society, "God-forbid", Shmaya convinced my folks to let him be a part of the plan to save my soul. They came to the decision that mum and dad would send me to a religious boarding school where he was going to be teaching - in Brazil, of all places.

Looking back, I'm unsure if Brazil was really the best place to send a teenage boy you were trying to keep away from women and music. But who am I to judge their desperate attempt at bringing a wayward child back to the path of righteousness?

At the age of 14, I was so unworldly that it was only after I had boarded the plane that it dawned on me that Brazil wasn't even in Australia. I must have fainted during that class in school.

It didn't worry me. In fact, knowing my parents would be on the other side of the planet, I had never felt so free.

I spent six months in São Paulo, barely studying and roaming the streets in my time off. I made friends with one military cop who must have been fascinated by what I was doing in town and how I didn't pay much attention to the dangers lurking in the streets.

I was utterly oblivious to the hazards of my new surroundings. It wasn't until after I had left that I heard that my principal's father had been shot dead during a street robbery gone wrong. Apparently, they killed him for less than $50.

After Shamaya's teaching contract ended in Brazil, my parents sent me to Minnesota in the United States, to try another religious boarding school, but this time without my big brother.

I was expelled within two weeks for allegedly refusing to obey many of the boarding school rules, an allegation I won't deny.

In a last-ditch effort to save my soul, my mother personally flew with me to Israel and dropped me at the only religious boarding school still willing to take me. If a sacred school in the Holy Land couldn't make me kosher, what could?

Walking into class on my first day, I wore the full religious uniform: an ultra-Orthodox Jewish black hat, white shirt, black pants and jacket with tzitzit (tassels) hanging out, the whole shtick.

But two days later, when it was confirmed that my mother was on a flight back to Australia, I walked out of my new school and headed straight to the local Arab market, where I found a hairdresser who agreed to bleach my head and shave off my sideburns. Then I was off to the piercing parlour for a stud in my left earlobe.

When I re-entered the dorm, the busy hall of almost a hundred loud teenage boys instantly fell eerily silent. You could have heard a pin drop as they all stared, trying to figure me out.

The shock on their faces all said the same thing: "Who?! What?! When?! Why?! Is that the Australian guy who just joined? What has he done?!".

I loved it.

The rosh yeshiva (school principal) directed me to his office, where he called my uncle, a known Rabbi in my mother's city of Kfar Saba.

The windows of the rosh yeshiva's office were full of teenage faces squished against them, peering in, trying to hear what was transpiring.

My uncle was kind to me on the phone, so I promised him I'd take public transport back to my grandmother's home in Kfar Saba.

On the train, I met a group of Rabbis from our same Chabad community, so I knew how to talk to them. Once I told them my story, they invited me to come and be a guest at their Chabad House, a Synagogue they used for their outreach work.

I thought that was a better option than facing my disappointed family. So I went with them.

When we got to the Chabad House, they called my big brother Yanki, who was serving as a soldier in the Israeli Army at the time.

Yanki, almost six years older than me, came to visit the next evening when Shabbat (the Sabbath) ended. He was in a green military uniform, with his M-16 strapped over his shoulder. He asked me if I wanted to stay or return to Kfar Saba with him.

He was too cool for me not to want to hang out with, so off we went.

Needless to say, I was back in Australia shortly after that.

But I wasn't done with being kicked out of schools. I was only just getting started.

Having worn out my welcome in Brazil, the US, and Israel, I arrived back in Melbourne to find I had worn out my welcome there too.

Dad gave me a choice. I could stay home and comply with the family's religious rules and regulations or make my own arrangements.

Well, I wasn't interested in religion, so it wasn't really a choice, was it?

I decided to take my chances on the street. I quickly discovered that while the freedom was incredible, the conditions were – shall we say - less than desirable. Sleeping in parks was uncomfortable and cold. I needed a plan.

In the Chabad community, it was imperative to bring Jews back into the fold of religion. That's why the guys in Israel were so willing to take me in. So, I approached a local Rabbi who ran a Chabad House for Israelis travelling through Australia. I figured he would see me as an opportunity to do some good.

Instead of telling him I was sleeping rough (in other words homeless); I said I had been dwelling with people who were not Jewish. And as I'd predicted, he immediately insisted I stay with him.

"Okay, if you insist," I replied. As if I was giving up on the comfort of my situation to surround myself with his positive spiritual influence.

My plan had worked.

I lived with him until Anglicare, an Anglican welfare agency got involved, placing me into foster care.

Remember how I told you I would lay in bed imagining how much better life would have been had I been adopted? Well, foster care wasn't exactly what I had envisaged.

Tova was the special lady who fostered me. She has remained a close friend and I love visiting her with my own children these days.

She wasn't used to fostering teens, especially out-of-control ones like me. But Tova persevered until I crossed a line she couldn't deal with - I got arrested.

It was a Sunday morning, and I was doing my weekly clothes shopping the only way I could afford, as I wasn't old enough to qualify for welfare payments yet.

I took the train from Balaclava Station and arrived at Richmond, where Dimmeys, the one and only clothes shop I knew, was located.

Dressed in a thick puffer jacket and baggy pants, I searched the store for my desired items.

Then in the changing room, I wore the t-shirts, the jumpers and the pants in layers before putting my puffer jacket and baggy pants back on over the top.

I must have looked ridiculous scurrying out of the store, especially because it was way too hot to wear the puffer jacket that day, let alone the rest of the clothes. It must have looked like I was on my way to the Winter Olympics.

Five meters from the door, two security guards grabbed me and walked me back into the shop. One on each side, the guards frog-marched me to the security office out the back.

"You know why you're here, mate," one guard told me.

"No I don't," I pretended.

"Come on, mate, we know what you've done," he insisted.

"Police are on the way," he added.

My gig was up.

Dimmey's security issued me a lifetime ban from all their stores, which I wouldn't admit then, hurt because of the fond memories of shopping there as a young child with my mother.

The police arrested me and took me back to Richmond Police Station, where they confiscated the stolen clothes, charged and released me.

I laughed as I walked out of the station, thinking the joke was on them because the puffer jacket and baggy pants I was still wearing, I had stolen from Dimmey's the previous week.

Understandably, my getting arrested was just too much for poor Tova. So, Gary, my social worker from Anglicare, organised for me to move into my first group home.

It was a Jewish Care home (A Jewish welfare agency) for troubled teens. The carers would cook and care for us as if we were their children. At the time, I had no idea how good I had it compared to what was to come.

I stayed at the Jewish Care home for about a year until it closed. Then I was introduced to the public system, which was an enormous reality check. It was there I encountered kids with shocking life stories and carers who didn't care much, as well as being exposed to hard drugs and violence.

Every day in the public system forced me to grow up five times faster than a boy should. I learnt daily life lessons in the most brutal ways.

On my first day in this government subsidised group home, I was a naive kid who wanted to be friends with everyone. One of my new roommates quickly taught me that it wasn't safe to trust anyone.

There were four of us in the room. I can't remember the others. I only remember scruffy Pete with a shaved head, who befriended me and asked to borrow my favourite hoodie.

"Here you go, just get it back to me tonight," I said as I handed him my prized possession.

"For sure matie," Pete said.

I got back to the home as soon as it opened at 4pm, and Pete, who was a couple of years older than me, hadn't returned yet.

Pete stumbled in at about 5.30pm, no longer wearing my hoodie.

"Hey mate, can I have my hoodie back?" I asked.

"What hoodie?" Pete replied.

"The one I lent you this morning," I answered innocently.

"I don't know what you're talking about mate," he said.

"I lent it to you this morning!" I protested.

Instantly Pete jumped in my face. I could smell his breath of decaying teeth.

"Are you calling me a thief? I'll stab ya, cunt," he shouted as spit flew from his mouth.

I was gutted. Not just because I was a germaphobe with stinky and likely diseased mouth juices all over my face. I loved that hoodie and was banned from returning to Dimmey's to get another. But what hurt even more was the betrayal of my new "friend".

Since that day, I have never trusted anyone simply on their word. It has served me well, particularly in my line of work. Being cynical means, I'm constantly questioning things. I owe scruffy Pete one for that.

Even with these blunt crash courses in life, I still preferred living in the public housing system over returning home to the forced religious way of life.

I became more street-smart.

I wasn't tough like some of those I lived with, or as we called it 'staunch', but I became resourceful.

One day, there was a religious event in Caulfield Park where many teenagers, not necessarily even Jewish, were hanging around on the outskirts. I was drinking vodka from a water bottle when police patrolling the area approached me.

"Hey you, what's in that bottle?" an officer asked.

"Water," I answered with a grin.

"Let me smell it," the officer demanded.

At that moment, I looked around and realised this was my chance. I feared getting into altercations with the 'Pete's' of the street because they could kill me. But by picking a fight with a cop, I would gain 'street cred', and anyway, I thought, "what was the worst the police would do to me?"

So, I tossed the vodka in the officer's face.

"OOOOOOH!" the crowd went nuts.

As the police tackled me, I threw a couple of pathetic swings towards the officers. These were not intended to hurt them, it was really more for my audience to spread the word.

I copped a well-deserved little beating that night, but the word undoubtedly spread.

My reputation often preceded me, and I became known as the crazy kid who wasn't even scared of the police.

It helped a lot.

But not always.

A couple of months later, a group called The Prahran Boys jumped me on a tram. They punched, kicked and stomped on me as retaliation for using my newly found tough facade on the wrong person.

Luckily, an older member of their group who recognised me from Little Hustlers, a local amusement arcade, stepped in to save me.

He managed to push the mob off me and pulled me up, helping me leave the tram.

I walked away with a bruised body and an even more bruised ego. But I got off lightly because the same group stabbed another kid two tram stops later.

Once I had learnt those brutal street lessons, surviving as a teen wasn't particularly difficult. That was, before the drugs took hold of me.

By fifteen or sixteen, the generous government (with taxpayers dollars) began paying for housing and welfare on the condition I was in school. So, I beat the system by getting kicked out of all three schools the social workers arranged. That was a total of six schools that expelled me here and overseas. I mucked up so severely that the worst schools eventually refused to enrol me.

Ironically, I would still hang out around schools because that's where all the kids were.

Once school wasn't an option, I had to become an active job seeker to qualify for support. And like most government programs, milking the system was easy.

On my first meeting, the careers counsellor informed me of the $500 budget to buy clothes to help make me presentable while looking for work.

The following week we planned to shop, but when I arrived, she couldn't find the money envelope in her drawer.

At first, she politely asked if I'd taken it when she left me alone in the room.

I hadn't. I never stole from family, friends or people that helped me. I couldn't do that.

But she didn't believe me, and why would she?

She was used to dealing with ratty little kids who would sell their own mother for ten dollars.

Being accused of a petty crime I hadn't committed hurt a lot. I really just wanted the careers counsellor to believe me, but couldn't convince her. Hopefully, she's reading this, remembers the incident, and now knows that I never stole that money.

My sense of morality was utterly messed up. When you've been taught that breaking the Sabbath is the worst thing you can do, getting drunk and taking drugs doesn't seem that bad by comparison.

Put it this way, smoking pot felt a lot less like a sin than eating pork.

So, I convinced myself that doing drugs was really not that bad. And besides, I wasn't keeping the Sabbath or eating Kosher anyway. So, if I was already committing the worst sins, a few more were hardly going to hurt.

The first time I remember smoking pot was when I was 14. I was hanging out at Little Hustlers, the local arcade frequented by all sorts of unsavoury types, which was probably why I liked chilling there. I was fascinated just watching the passing parade of humanity.

One day two girls, 18 and 19 years old, asked me if I smoked weed.

"Of course," I replied with typical bravado, even though I didn't.

"Do you want to come back to our place for a bong?"

"Sure," I said, having no idea what a "bong" even was.

I don't know why I went with those girls. They weren't clean, and they weren't pretty. But they were older than me and had this air of confidence that intrigued me, so I went with them.

Once at their ramshackle place, I hardly sucked down a single cone and was on my ass, completely stoned.

Lying on the bed, one of the girls started touching me and asked if I wanted to have sex.

"Fine, but I'm not doing anything," I answered her.

The truth is I had no idea what to do. It was my first time, and I'd never attended a single sex ed class. In fact, it wasn't that long ago that I thought you prayed to God for kids. One of my classmates had to point out that my parents didn't just 'pray' seventeen times before I realised something else was going on!

Anyway, the next thing I knew, two over-age girls were taking turns having sex with me.

When I straightened up, I ran to my friend's house as quickly as possible. I couldn't wait to tell him that I'd lost my virginity.

"Aaron, Aaron," I yelled as I knocked on his door.

"I'm coming," Aaron answered in a far less enthusiastic tone as he slowly walked down the hallway towards me.

"Bro, you won't believe what just happened!" I shouted.

"Ok, I'm coming. What happened?" He asked, a little more excited as he flung the door open.

"You gotta promise not to tell anyone." Making him swear before I divulged what had happened.

"Ok. You have my word," Aaron vowed.

It wasn't that I was embarrassed by losing my virginity, I just didn't want anyone to know who I'd lost it with.

"I just had sex!" I blurted out as his mother appeared behind him, thankfully not paying any attention.

"What?! With who?" now whispering, as excited as I was.

"You swear not to tell anyone?" I double checked we were clear on the terms.

"I already promised!" He assured me.

But he lied.

The next time I walked into Little Hustlers, where I'd met these girls, everyone started clapping and laughing.

"Why are you all laughing?" I asked.

"Aaron told us that you've been a naughty kid".

And a few weeks later, the rumour apparently started by the girls was that I "didn't know how to use it".

No shit. I'm not sure what they were expecting when they drugged and (technically) raped a 14-year-old kid.

And the pot that they introduced me to quickly became a friend, who then almost as promptly introduced me to a long and unsavoury list of associates.

I was soon attending raves and doing party drugs like ecstasy and speed. The MDMA from the pills gave me this "loving" feeling, and the amphetamine kept my energy going so I could party all night.

When my tolerance for the speed grew, diminishing the effect, I swapped it for ice which would keep me going from Thursday night until Sunday.

I had transformed from a kid living at home, where even the television was regulated by strict observance of religion, into a teenager living from one long weekend to the next.

One night my friend showed me how much more effective ice was when you injected it rather than burn it.

The high was an instant rush, and I never turned back after injecting it for the first time. I injected everything, even the ecstasy pills I'd crush and inject.

But, as the old expression goes, what goes up must come down - and the come-downs were dreadful. I'd be depressed from Monday until Wednesday, sweating the drugs out with a lack of appetite and an aching body.

It was then that another friend introduced me to the "magic solution".

"This will fix your come-down, but promise me you'll never bang [inject] it," he told me on a Monday after one of our typical weekends.

"I promise," I responded.

Burning it on silver foil, as I used to do with the ice worked. Within minutes my come down was gone.

I had just had my first taste of heroin.

"Let me take a little home so I can sleep," I begged him.

"Sure, but don't bang it in your arm," he warned me again.

"Of course," I nodded back.

But I knew I was lying.

As soon as I got home, I got a spoon, syringe, alcohol wipe, cotton ball and water. I sanitised the spoon and added a little rock in there. Then I used the syringe plunger to crush the rock, before adding some water and mixed it until it was liquid. I took a tiny ball of cotton, dropped it in the liquid, and sucked the fluid through the cotton, so it filtered what I was going to stick in my body.

I tied a belt around my bicep and, piercing the needle into the popping vein, drew back a drop of blood to ensure I was in the right spot. Then I pushed the liquid straight into my vein.

I could feel it travel up my arm and straight to my head.

It was the best feeling of my entire life. It was the most potent painkiller I'd ever experienced - physically and mentally. And I was clearly in a lot of pain.

I didn't know it yet, but from that day, I was 15 years old and addicted to heroin.

For months I continued my routine of taking party drugs from Thursday to Sunday, and recovering on Monday.

But my recovery had become fun. So much so that I looked forward to that more than the partying.

One day, I thought to myself, let's just skip the middleman and go straight for the dope.

I never meant for any of it to happen. It was a simple case of one door opening to another and another until, eventually, I was a long way from home, at least metaphorically.

But no matter how deep into drugs I got, I always told myself that it was just a passing phase and that I could snap out of it whenever I wanted.

The people around me were really screwed up, but I convinced myself that I was different. In quiet moments I assured myself that I could walk home anytime I wanted and go straight back to the safety, if not rigidity, of religion.

This, of course, was hypocritical since I had no interest in religion. And yet it was this religious get-out-of-jail-free card - kept in my back pocket and able to be played at any time - that enabled me to exist in a crazy world of drugs and petty crime without ever becoming completely lost in it.

As a full-on heroin addict, I would frequent houses where junkies had needles strewn about the floor and yet, somehow convinced myself that I wasn't really part of it.

The addicts I called friends were godless. I had a religious upbringing.

They had abandoned themselves to addiction and the ravages that went with it. I was a germaphobe who insisted everything needed to be clean.

To keep my habit going, I started selling drugs and committing crime.

I began with petty stuff like creating fake vouchers from Chadstone, a large shopping mall. We'd buy things using fake coupons and ensure the change was a maximum of seventy dollars, so they'd give it in cash. And then we'd sell the items.

Not surprisingly, after a while, I got caught. At my hearing, I walked into the court with my stylish Hugo Boss suit I had bought using our same dodgy vouchers, and as if for my joy, the magistrate opened with, "nice suit."

I turned and winked at my mate sitting a few rows behind me, who was also grinning ear to ear.

Petty crime escalated to more serious stuff like armed robbery, which sounds drastic, but it was rolling other kids by lying to them that I had a knife.

I never physically hurt anyone because I couldn't. My heart couldn't bear inflicting pain on an innocent person. Pretending to be badass to bully them for their belongings was hard enough.

Even so, I felt more guilty about breaking the Sabbath than robbing people.

It was as if I was passing through a strange land as a tourist, tasting the local fare but never forgetting that I came from somewhere else. Provided I never lost the memory of where I was from, I would never lose myself.

I thought freedom was the absence of any boundaries, and so I exercised my freedom to its fullest extent until, ironically, I was sabotaging my own freedom through drugs and the court system.

At one point, I was purposely breaching my probation orders, so they'd lock me up. A judge ordered me to sign in at Caulfield Police Station three times a week, so I deliberately didn't show up for a month.

When I finally did attend, I informed the cop that I had breached my orders and told him that they should lock me up. But they didn't. Instead, to my incredible frustration, they just warned me not to do it again.

I'd leave the cop shop disappointed and relieved at the same time. I wanted them to jail me for the street cred. But in all honesty, I wasn't sure I would survive it.

CHAPTER THREE

TOUCH ROCK BOTTOM

Party drugs, usually a concoction of MDMA for the lovey-dovey feeling, topped with a bit of methamphetamine to power me on all night, didn't affect me adversely compared to opioids. I would get high, then come down, and let my body recover before taking them all over again. Heroin, however, would not leave me alone.

The worst it ever got was after a massive weekend bender on party drugs, during which time I had not slept at all. I was found by a support worker, sitting in a shared public youth house with the other two kid occupants, arguing in gibberish.

All three of us had gone into a drug-induced psychosis, compounded by a lack of sleep. The support worker organised for us to be put straight into detox, which was always a great 14-day cleanse to knock your tolerance down and start again.

Heroin was different though. I was unable to function without it. Once addicted, I was no longer taking heroin to experience a euphoric high, I was now using it to feel normal.

I had reached a point where I didn't give a shit about life. I became estranged from my family and girlfriend, the only things I owned were mostly stolen clothes and crappy electronics. All I thought about was heroin. It had become all-consuming.

In fact, I was so afraid of the physical pain of withdrawal from the drug that I started preparing needles in advance so that I wouldn't even have to wait five minutes to get my next hit when needed.

Unlike the party drugs, the addiction was more physical than anything. With party drugs, I needed to stop, let my body recover, and then start again which was why detoxing was so helpful. But heroin was the opposite. I physically needed more, incrementally, each day.

And when I didn't have enough, I would get sick, I mean, really sick. Imagine the worst flu you've ever had. Now, multiply that by a hundred and that's still probably only half. It was debilitating. At times I couldn't even move.

I'd been sharing a bed with my mate at his place for a few months because I didn't have the energy or motivation to find my own home.

One night, I prepared a needle for the following morning and put it on a coffee table in the middle of his room, about five metres from the bed. When I woke the next day in agony, I literally had to crawl across the floor to get to it.

There I was, dragging myself across the dirty floor of a junkie's bedroom to stick a needle in my arm just so I could feel normal again.

It worked.

Remember the flu you just imagined? Now just think a doctor administered a magical medicine. As the drug travelled up your arm, within moments, you were better.

That was my high.

It was at that moment that I realised I had hit rock bottom. I mean, there was no lower point than that.

It was time for me to play my get-out-of-jail-free card.

Holding my head down in shame, I slowly walked to my parent's house, only two blocks away and knocked on the door. I felt like a complete stranger standing on those familiar steps, waiting for someone to answer, praying for a lifeline.

Mum opened the door, and upon seeing her, my emotions burst. I cried my eyes out for the first time since leaving home a few years ago. As for her, I cannot even imagine what she must have been feeling.

Standing before her was her 10th child - now 17-years-old - dirty, sad, covered in acne and frightfully skinny.

I must have been a miserable sight, dressed in tattered, stinky clothes that hung off my malnourished frame. I was a complete mess.

I may have rejected my parents' religion, but I knew my mother would always be there with open arms when I needed her. And I needed her now.

My father was less emotional. He "had to ask the Rabbi" if I could stay because I wasn't practicing the faith.

Thank God the Rabbi's advice was, if it's life and death, they must help me. Dad called our family doctor, who was also from the ultra-orthodox community.

Within moments of our consultation, the doctor ruled my condition as life and death.

With rabbinic approval and medical advice, I detoxed in my room for an excruciatingly long two weeks. Meanwhile, my parents moved heaven and earth to get me into a rehabilitation program. I'd previously been in and out of detox and rehab centres, usually by court order. I'd never minded going because I had always seen rehab both as a way to knock down my tolerance and also it was the perfect networking opportunity.

But this time, I was determined to take rehabilitation seriously. The alternative was too dreadful to even contemplate.

I'd become a junkie, something I never believed could happen to me.

After three hard going months in drug rehab, I felt like a new man. Could I have come to my senses earlier? Probably. But our system seemed designed to enable junkie juveniles.

Social workers were too easily manipulated by a kid who learnt quickly how to game the system. And police - even back then - would never hold me accountable because they'd back off immediately as soon as I played the race card.

One time, early in my drug habit, when I was still dealing pills to get me by, the police stopped me for a random search. I had been walking with a mate to my government housing down South Road in Moorabbin and had a pack of a hundred ecstasy pills in my bag.

As soon as they pulled up, I began ranting about how the police were only targeting me because I was an Arab. So instead of continuing with their plan, they got defensive and denied it, saying they were only searching my mate, who was an Aussie.

We laughed about it all the way home because, unlike me, he had no drugs on him at all.

I can't help but think now about how different things might have turned out if the police hadn't backed down. Would I have gotten as far with my addiction if authorities had stopped me in my tracks?

I probably needed someone – whether a rabbi, a foster parent, a police officer or a magistrate – to go much harder on me. Not that I blame any of them for where I ended up. I made choices, many of which I wish I could go back and undo. Hindsight and growing up - as they say - is a beautiful thing.

I have learnt, however, that even your worst moments can have a redeeming effect if you learn from them. Nothing gives you empathy for others like having touched rock bottom with the soles of your own wayward feet, and nothing builds character like climbing your way up from the pit of despair.

A burning desire to be in the spotlight, my larrikin attitude, combined with an incurable curiosity, a willingness to take risks and a natural disdain for authority – traits that had taken me to the depths of misery, were the exact same things that would, paradoxically, within a few years, take me to great heights.

But first, my wayward talents needed to be redirected. And where better to do that than in the Israeli Defence Force?

Some weeks into my voluntary rehab, I began the process of making Aliyah (immigrating to Israel), so I could enlist in the Israel Defence Force (IDF).

I wanted to join the Israeli army because I feared that, with the way my life had been going up to this point, the only alternative was I'd end up overdosing or in jail.

Two of my brothers had done military time in the Holy Land. As the Jewish state meant so much to my identity and I'd always dreamed of following in their footsteps. Besides, what else was I going to do?

I considered joining the Australian army, but after attending an information session, it was clear that my criminal history made that problematic. Becoming an Israeli citizen and joining the IDF gave me a clean slate and a fresh start, with authorities in Israel not knowing about my delinquent past.

Plus, if I'd joined the Australian army, I'd have been shipped off to fight someone else's war. Whereas in Israel, I'd be defending the lives of my family and my people.

Israel's Defence Force (IDF) only accepts international volunteers to join specific, non-elite units, which I didn't want to serve in. Or at least that's how it was in 2004. So, making Aliyah, which means immigrating to Israel, and becoming a citizen, was the only way I could join the Golani Brigade.

Golani is recognised as the most fierce brigade in the Israeli army. Israelis often joke that Golani soldiers are sent in first to draw out the enemy, giving up their positions so the Airforce can finish the job.

Unlike its mostly Ashkenazi (Jews of European descent) paratrooper rival, the Golani Brigade was majority Sephardi (Spanish, North African, and Middle Eastern Jews). So, with a Yemenite background, I'd fit right in.

My brothers and entire extended family served in Golani. The only person who didn't was mum's brother, uncle Shaul, who was killed as a paratrooper in the 1967 Six-Day War. So, signing up for anything else was out of the question.

I arrived in Israel in 2005, aged 19. I was immediately put into an absorption centre to live with primarily Eastern European and Ethiopian immigrants. My roommate was the only other Aussie in town, and we spent the days studying Hebrew and the nights touring local bars. The army said I had to be there a year before I could join the military.

Knowing my school history, even though they stuck me in a class with 16 Russian girls, lasting a year seemed unlikely.

I quickly made a friend who worked for The Jewish Agency (an international organisation for new immigrants) at the absorption centre who was willing to lobby the IDF on my behalf to let me commence my service early.

The IDF called me in to do a Hebrew test, but I failed miserably. I'd never spoken Hebrew at home. My parents sometimes used it to talk among themselves, so we wouldn't understand.

My only knowledge of Hebrew was from learning Torah (The Old Testament) as a kid – but the Torah is written in ancient Hebrew. Imagine a new immigrant arriving in Australia and attempting to communicate in Shakespeare's English. That was me in Israel.

Suffice to say, I was mocked a lot.

The IDF finally did agree for me to join an early intake, on the condition that I spend my first three months in a military school for the intensive study of Hebrew. Of course, I enthusiastically agreed.

So off I went to the induction base near Tel Aviv, called Bakum, to do all the paperwork and medical examinations.

To get into the unit I wanted, I had to achieve a medical profile score of at least 72 out of a possible 97. A score of 82 would have meant

I could join special forces, but 72 would be enough to qualify me for combat service in all other combat units.

The IDF intake doctor scored me the minimum 72 score I required. I'd like to think I could have gotten higher if it weren't for an incident during my party days where I had sustained a severe injury after walking out of a moving van while high on drugs. That mishap resulted in surgery that left me with thirty-nine pins in my left shoulder – not ideal for a wannabe Rambo.

To celebrate qualifying for combat, I went out for a drinking session with my Australian absorption centre flatmate. Not that we needed an excuse to go out drinking. Unlike me, Daniel was based in Israel to play soccer.

When we got home, being drunk and acting a fool, I attempted a fly kick that I had no idea how to execute. I soon learnt that being accepted into combat doesn't make you Rambo.

I landed badly. Very badly.

My leg puffed up, and no matter how elevated or how tight I wrapped the compression bandage, or how much ice I applied, the swelling would not subside.

Two days later, my uncle forced me to get it x-rayed. I didn't want to because I couldn't afford my medical profile to drop any further.

I explained my conundrum to the doctor, who now appeared as invested as me in a good outcome of my silly night out.

Walking into his office to get the results, the doctor asked, "so what do you think, is it broken?"

"No way," I answered with probably much more hope than belief.

"100% broken," my uncle Yoel who had brought me there, chimed in.

Yoel is my mother's most religious sibling, so it felt like a divine premonition. He said it with such authority, it sounded like God told him directly.

Sure enough, the doctor put me out of misery. Well, the misery of not knowing and into a new misery of doubt for my military future.

"You've destroyed your ankle. You broke it in several places, and a cast won't work as you've also torn all the surrounding ligaments," he said in a tone that simultaneously sounded disappointed for my military crisis but impressed by my ability to minimise such a severe injury.

"Urgent surgery is your only option," he added.

Within days a large rod and four bolts were implanted above my left ankle.

Luckily, I had about fourteen weeks until my military Hebrew course began, and the surgeon promised my plaster could come off in twelve.

I still had hope to hold onto. Surely, two weeks after removing the cast should be enough for me to learn to walk perfectly again? Rambo had way worse injuries to recover from between sequels.

The first eleven weeks felt like months, the next seven days felt like weeks, and the last hours went so slowly they felt like days. But finally, my cast came off.

As the surgeon cut the plaster from my leg and foot, I could see how skinny I had become. It looked gross and didn't smell great, either. But worse, once the cast was off, I could not put much weight on my foot at all.

At that moment, I felt sick, thinking my entire combat service would be rendered impossible.

The surgeon must have sensed my desperation and offered me an air cast ankle brace I could hide in my shoe, at least for the first few months.

I cannot tell you how relieved I was. I would have done pretty much anything to get to Golani.

The ankle brace made it bearable to limp from the surgeon's office. He advised walking on it as much as possible to strengthen the muscles.

Walking became my only mission. It was my pre-army training.

For two weeks, I walked everywhere. It was agonising at first, but then the pain began to subside, and I could feel the muscles re-building.

Finally, the day had come. I boarded the bus, and for the first and possibly last time in my life, I tried to blend in without being noticed. I didn't want any attention so no one would see my limp.

But coming off that bus on my first day, a commanding officer instantly noticed my abnormal walk. My dragging left leg betrayed me no matter how hard I tried to hide it. In perfect English, she asked what was wrong with my foot.

"Oh, that's nothing. I twisted my ankle over the weekend, but it'll be fine," I answered.

"Okay, but if it doesn't get better, go see the base doctor," she ordered.

And just like that, my first hurdle in the Israeli Army was avoided like a pro.

My Hebrew, however, was not going as well as my foot. I would eventually experience combat, but honestly, those three months of learning Hebrew were the most challenging part of the army.

You have to remember that I had never managed to pass anything at school. The only thing I perfected at school was the art of getting expelled. And yet, here I was, back in a classroom.

It didn't feel like I was in the real army - sitting in a language school for 12 weeks - while being mistreated and having to cop it. It was basically three months of constantly being barked at by a bunch of 18-year-old power-hungry commanders with no combat experience or even training.

It was terrible.

And my Hebrew didn't get much better. But at least it gave my foot time to heal.

Eleven weeks in, the induction unit visited our base for a personal interview with each soldier regarding the future of our service.

This is where they decide our fate.

"Please sit," the sergeant instructed, pointing to a chair on the opposite side of the table.

"Your medical profile is 72, which means you can join a combat unit," he said as I was taking my seat.

"Is that what you want to do in your service?" he asked.

"Yes sir," I responded enthusiastically.

"Okay. What are your top three choices of unit you'd like to serve in?" he asked.

"Golani, top. Golani, second. Golani, third," I replied cheekily.

"You understand that whatever unit we allocate, you must go there?" he said in a firm voice.

"Let me be clear," I told him equally firmly. "If the sign on the bus doesn't say Golani, I ain't getting on it."

"They'll send you to military jail if you refuse to follow an order to get on a bus," he warned.

"You think I'm scared of going to jail? I flew from the other side of the world to join Golani. So it's either going to be Golani or jail. You choose," I confidently answered.

He must have thought I was made of the right stuff, because I was the only one in my class of thirty soldiers who chose Golani and got in.

Basic training was ruthless; twelve weeks of pure pain. But I loved every minute of it.

Towards the end, an officer caught me wearing the air cast ankle brace and made me explain myself. I said it just helped me to run better, to which he reacted by ripping it off me and throwing it in the bin.

"In Golani we rely on ourselves to get the job done," he declared.

Thank goodness I didn't really need it anymore. He did me a favour, as I had been wearing it out of baseless fear. My ankle was healed. The brace was likely doing more harm than good in not allowing my muscles to fully activate. But it was a habit giving me a false sense of security which I wasn't prepared to break myself.

If my officer hadn't forced me to "man up" that day, I would possibly still be wearing that silly thing today.

Being the class clown helped me get through training, and I'd like to think it made things fun for my comrades and commanding officers as well.

A typical punishment I would receive for making everyone laugh at inappropriate times was to run around the barracks within sixty seconds.

It was a standard punishment.

They wouldn't time you. Instead, it was the new recruit's job to count out loud as he ran.

Most soldiers counted slowly to ensure they made it within the sixty seconds given. Not me. I counted super-fast, making sure it took me at least sixty-five seconds to have a laugh at the end.

My commanders would make me run around the barracks over and over, promising not to let me stop until I made the time. But I refused to give him the satisfaction. Collapsing was my preferred choice. And then they'd promise to continue it later.

I could always see their smirk.

Everyone could see it.

The look on their faces always said, "Why is this Australian such a nut?" I wouldn't be surprised if the commanders secretly bet on who would break me.

I would have loved to be in on that action. I'd have cleaned up as they all failed.

One time after we finally got to sleep at about 2am, our sergeant woke me up and demanded I start running - around the barracks, bear crawls in the mud, dry drills with my m-16. It was relentless.

But none of it ever came close to breaking my spirit. What it did do was help me to earn their respect.

Advanced training, however, was more mentally taxing. My body was broken by that point, and my spirit was running thin. Like most of my peers, I was close to giving up several times. But somehow, I didn't.

My three years of military service were split in two, punctuated by a quick trip home to Australia.

CHAPTER FOUR

SEEKING SALVATION
IN ZION

A year in, Israeli forces had suffered some bad defeats in Lebanon, so the decision was made to put the whole army through special retraining. The last thing I wanted was to go back into training, so when our unit was chosen to go first, I immediately applied for the two weeks leave international soldiers are entitled to.

It was during those two weeks back in Australia that I met Sarah, who would become my first wife. Sarah was childhood friends with my cousin and spoke some Portuguese. I needed a translator to help me communicate with a dodgy travel agent I had met when I was in Brazil years earlier.

Sarah was mid-moving house. In return for her linguistic services, Sarah conscripted my help building her and her kids' furniture in their new home.

Sarah was six years older than me and had two children from a previous relationship that she had described as awful. The more she talked about how horrible and abusive her last relationship had been, the more I wanted to help her. I was a 20-year-old Jewish kid with a saviour complex. Looking back, I think I more or less talked myself into a relationship I didn't really want and certainly didn't need. I lacked an understanding of the gravity of committing to marriage and how it would set the trajectory of my life.

What I wasn't prepared to admit then was that Sarah was perfect for someone, that person just wasn't me.

I knew that inherently in the pit of my stomach.

When things were good between us, Sarah was great. We had fun times. I loved talking to her. It got me through dark army days. But I was a damaged kid who wasn't ready for what I was signing up for. I needed time to work myself out, not be a dad to two young children and a husband to their mother, whom I didn't really know.

When my parents discovered I was keen on a non-Jew who already had two children, they were utterly opposed. And by now, you know me well enough to know that their opposition only served to spur me on.

So instead of returning to the army for the post-Lebanon war retraining in Israel like I was supposed to, I decided I wanted to stay and pursue the forbidden relationship.

First, I had to try to extend my two-week leave. There was no way I was going back to that body and spirit-breaking three-month training if I could avoid it.

I called the Israeli consulate in Canberra, which had the authority to issue me a fortnight extension at home without any genuine excuse.

Frank, a long-time friend, floated the idea of working with him for a month in scrap metal. We'd make enough money to holiday in Thailand before travelling to Israel together. Frank was also friends with my little brother Chaim who lived with me in Israel.

So the plan was set. Work in Melbourne, then go MIA in Thailand until training was over. Then I would return to Israel with Frank. From there he would then hang out with my little bro while I faced the consequences of this devious plan.

Frank and I worked hard for that entire month but played even harder for a few weeks in Pattaya before returning to Israel.

Before we headed to Thailand, I caught up with an old friend. We'd been close mates for years, and our bond was even more potent as we were the only people in our circle to successfully beat heroin. Ironically, we decided for old-time's sake, to use this opportunity to give heroin one last taste while I was back in town.

Excitedly we scored and went back to his home to "wack the smack". At least, that's how we described injecting heroin.

I vaguely remember sitting at his computer selecting music when I felt that I needed to lie down. The next thing I knew, paramedics were working on me on my way to the hospital.

My friend had gone to the bathroom when he noticed I was lying lifeless on the spare mattress, so he called the ambulance.

The paramedics administered Narcan, a powerful drug, which swiftly reverses the effects of the opioids. It sucked being pulled back to earth from what felt like heaven. But you wouldn't be reading my story now if he hadn't called for help that day.

That was the last time I ever relapsed. Even then, I knew I had too much to live for.

The next three weeks of partying in Pattaya, for starters.

Before leaving Bangkok for Tel Aviv, I packed a suitcase full of cigarette cartons, the best currency in the army. I thought it was an excellent investment at about $10 a carton in Thailand instead of $100 each in Israel. My only challenge would be getting them into the country.

When we landed in Israel, customs officials opened my bag and looked at me in shock.

"There's a limit of two cartons per person," the officer declared. "You have 50!"

"I'm a lone soldier from Australia, volunteering in Golani to defend Israel. I can't afford cigarettes here. So unless you're willing to buy them for me, I'm taking these cartons with me," I answered.

"Golani? Thank you for your service, soldier," he replied as he zipped up the bag and passed it straight back to me.

With all their faults, Israelis treat their combat soldiers as heroes. As they should. And if you travel there to serve, the people love you.

As planned, I dropped Frank off with my little brother and returned to base as the post-Lebanon war retraining ended.

My two weeks of authorised time off had turned into three months, during which time none of my army friends imagined I would ever come back. When I returned, it was, to them, as if a ghost had just walked through the gates.

But I wasn't going to miss active duty for the world. Especially as we were being stationed in Gaza, which guaranteed action.

As I entered the barracks on Thursday, my officer was fuming. He told me I was to be confined to kitchen duties until Monday, when he assured me in no uncertain terms that I would be court-martialed.

I spent the weekend on base catching up with friends and handing out cigarettes like Robin Hood, sharing the spoils of crime with the most desperate in society.

Soldiers started betting on how much jail time I would receive for going MIA in Thailand. Most thought I would be facing between three to five months, which would then be added to my compulsory service time.

When the day of my court-martial arrived, there was enormous excitement in the air and, of course, plenty of cigarettes being passed around.

The line outside Military Court on a Monday morning at any Golani base is always long. But there was only one matter anyone cared about on that particular day. Even those lining up to have their own cases heard were more interested in what would happen to the crazy Aussie who was always good for a joke and a free cigarette.

I walked into the makeshift courtroom and stood before the Regiment Commander, whom, I have to admit, was a most daunting figure. The dude was scary.

Stories about this Regiment Commander from people who were in Lebanon with him a few months back demanded respect. He was, by all accounts, a fearless fighter and his presence wasn't any less intimidating. He was a behemoth of a man with a deep voice that made me feel like an insignificant little child standing before him.

To his left was the super pissed Company Commander, who had authorised my two weeks of leave - a scary bloke in his own right. He'd received a Tzalash, the highest military honour, usually given to soldiers who are killed by an insane act of bravery.

He had received it for flipping a terrorist onto his own grenade after the terrorist pulled the pin. He then jumped on top of the terrorist while the grenade exploded beneath them—saving a dozen soldiers.

To the right sat another Company Commander. And at the end of the table, a high-ranking military social worker.

"You were missing in action for 10 weeks beyond your authorised two-week visit home. What do you have to say for yourself, soldier?" the Regiment Commander asked to begin the hearing.

"I got sick and received a two-week extension from the consulate, commander," I said as I handed over a certificate from the Israeli consulate in Canberra.

The Regiment Commander read the official document, looked up and said: "That explains two of the ten weeks. What about the other eight weeks?"

"Commander," I told him, "I had to work in Australia to make money to buy a new ticket back to Israel."

"As soon as I did, I jumped on a flight that stopped overnight in Thailand. But I woke up in the morning with food poisoning and could not even leave my room. It took me a few days to fully recover, but I needed a new ticket to Israel. I got a job in a bar while paying my living expenses and saving enough for a flight back. I finally managed to buy a ticket last week, and caught the first flight I could afford."

My fear of lying to his face must have made my story sound more believable because he responded by thanking me for going to such extraordinary lengths to return and volunteer.

"You could have stayed in the safety of Australia, but you chose to come and fight for the citizens of Israel. Thank you, soldier. You are dismissed," he said, ending the hearing.

I was in total shock.

As I walked out, the twenty or so soldiers waiting at the door all looked at me with questioning faces "nuuuu?" they said, meaning, come on, tell us what you got.

My face lit up as I signalled a zero and began to do a little dance.

"No, you're lying!" one soldier exclaimed in disbelief.

Another demanded, "How is that even possible? I got a month in jail for skipping two days!"

"Did you bribe him with cigarettes?" a witty soldier laughed.

And that's how I got the reputation as the Aussie who could get away with anything.

As I walked back to the barracks, the military social worker ran up behind me and said, "Avi, you are so full of shit. But well played!"

I liked her. She was cool. But she could read me like a book. I guess that's what made her so good at her job.

When I returned to the barracks, the Company Commander was waiting to let me know he'd moved to another company for the Gaza deployment.

He wasn't thrilled with the outcome of my hearing, to say the least.

But the change of company was perfect for me. My Platoon commander, Dudy, was a legend. He was a Christian Arab-Israeli who treated me like a brother.

Dudy would take me off base for Christian holidays to spend them with his family in the south of the country. He knew I was Jewish, but I guess being from Australia, he knew I was familiar with it all.

Let me tell you, nothing beats an Arab Christmas. The food was so bloody good. I'm getting hungry right now, just writing about it.

I was one of two marksmen in the class. Unlike a sniper, we worked within a team and used an M-4 with a Trijicon optic in daylight or night vision after dark. Our range was nowhere near a sniper's. We could hit a target up to a couple hundred meters.

Patrolling the Gaza-Israel border, a marksman probably sees the most action. From firing warning shots dispersing crowds heading towards the exclusion zone, to hitting terrorists trying to breach the security fence, it was the best job to have.

However, combat was the scariest thing you can imagine. Loud, outgoing kids, full of bravado like myself, talked a big game from the Israeli side of the fence before we were sent into Gaza. And then we absolutely shat ourselves as we were being shot at from close range.

In one operation, we entered Gaza under the cover of darkness, to take hold of a position terrorists were using to fire rockets at Israeli towns.

Our mission was to capture terrorists or, if engaged, to kill them. But they never showed.

After a couple of days, we began to withdraw. As our class marched towards the Israeli side, we were ambushed at close range in the trees just ahead of us.

They knew we were there, explaining why they never showed. Instead, they had waited in the bushes to attack us on our way out.

We all dropped to the ground and began returning fire.

The other marksman, who was at the front of our group and next to Dudy, was immediately hit by shrapnel. And then suddenly, from behind, we were copping long-range fire.

So there we were, ambushed in Gaza, being fired on from all sides, and my gun bloody jammed.

I had cleaned the M-4 before the mission. But the dirt of two days was too much for the piece of crap. It just wouldn't fire, and I couldn't unjam it without the unique tool.

It was one of the few times in my life that I've actually thought, "That's it. I'm dead", except for the time I really did die, but that comes later in the story.

I kept hurdling from one side to the other of a small sand dune, trying to take cover from the front and the back as bullets whizzed around me. I was cursing my M-4 in every language. It was the most helpless feeling in the world, being shot at and unable to shoot back.

Powerless, that is, until I heard the sweet sound of an Israeli chopper above, heading for the assholes shooting at us.

And as loud and sexy as that chopper sounded, it was nothing compared to the sound it made moments later launching rockets at the enemy – pop, pop, pop – and as quickly as we had been doomed, we were saved.

The gunshots ended, and I heard Dudy calling me to the front as the other marksman was injured.

We needed to check that the three terrorists in the trees ahead of us had been neutralised. This job was for a marksman with his commander, because both were equipped with night vision and a quick shot.

As I followed Dudy, I informed him that my gun was jammed.

"So why the hell did you come? Get back!" he ordered, as he went ahead to check the bodies himself.

Once cleared, Dudy marched us back to safety in Israel.

At the debrief, Dudy made a big deal out of me following him into danger without a functioning weapon. Painting me as a hero, saying I deserved to be honoured for it.

"Commander, I wasn't being brave. I was shitting myself. I was so scared that we would die out there tonight, and my body's survival mechanism was simply to follow orders," I said in protest.

I don't think he believed me. I got the feeling he thought I was being humble. I wasn't. I had never been so scared in my entire life.

The thing about combat is that it took me from a kid who had just run amok on the streets of Melbourne, fearing not much at all, to a young man shitting his pants, fearing certain death. It humbled me a little, and I needed that.

Moreover, experiencing combat took me from a kid who had no regard for authority – laughing at judges and hitting a police officer - to being desperate to follow orders because I knew that if I didn't, I wouldn't survive.

The other thing military service taught me was that there are often good people on both sides, trapped in a system they didn't create and that they can't escape.

I remember being at the Gaza border as a dad and his two children walked toward Israel, waving a white piece of cloth to signal to us that they wanted to come across.

And then, without warning, Hamas operatives started firing at them from behind. I'll never forget the look on that dad's face. He was terrified as he was being shot at by his own people. And all we could do was duck for cover as he ran towards us, shielding his precious kids and hoping like hell that they made it to Israel.

But here's the crazy thing. In the back of your mind, there was always the thought, that he could have been strapped with explosives. Did he want us to save him? Or was he wanting to kill us? You just never knew.

Using human shields, typically women and children has been a horrific but often-used terrorist tactic. It would always make us think twice about opening fire, and if we do decide to engage, a camera would often be ready to capture the "brutal murder" and disseminate it around the world.

This horror show was playing before my eyes in real-time. Should we help this father and his kids while they are being shot at? Or do we dive for cover to save ourselves?

Do we treat him as an innocent civilian? Or do we treat him as a combatant?

While most of us were ducking for cover, one fearless Ethiopian tracker in our unit walked straight toward the danger. He was happy to risk his life, betting the father and children were victims, and he got to them as it rained bullets around him. I'm pleased to say that he successfully rescued them.

Once safely in Israel, the Palestinian trio were handed over to Israeli intelligence. I have no idea what happened to them, but I'd like to think that the family ended up, like my commander, being able to build a new life in Israel with the other two million Arab-Israelis.

Israel was the chance for me to build a new life, or at least to escape my old one.

Soldiers often asked me, "Why the hell are you in the army fighting Hamas in Gaza rather than soaking up the sun at Bondi beach?"

It was a great question, and I had undoubtedly asked myself the same thing during those three months of language school and by the end of combat training.

However, I preferred to be in Gaza for most of my deployment than back home. It was often less chaotic than where I came from. But from time to time, being a soldier got annoying.

One night I was invited to a party in Jerusalem with a friend. We had to be back on base the following morning, so we'd planned to stay at the city's free lodging for soldiers.

We took our bags, dropped them off at the accommodation, and headed to the bar.

"You can't bring that in," a security guard told us, pointing at our rifles.

"Come on brother," I begged.

"I can't let you in with it. Go drop it off and come back," he insisted.

We walked a ten-minute walk back to where we were staying, only to be informed that the soldiers housing no longer had a gun safe available.

"Shit!" my frustrated friend reacted.

I was so annoyed. We had been super excited about this last night before we had to get back to work. It was supposed to be a great party.

"Should we hide them?" my mate asked as we walked back to our bunks, trying to figure out our next move.

I was tempted to say yes, but where? It's not like military rifles were easy to conceal. And the idea of them being stolen didn't bear thinking about. Even for me, the jail time wasn't worth it.

The room we were staying in had 12 beds, two of which had our bags on them already. Sitting on a bed tucked away in the corner of the room was a cadet who, from the look of his uniform, I could tell was in basic training.

"Soldier," I said in an authoritative voice.

"Yes, sir," the junior replied, immediately sitting up straight in acknowledgement that he was in the presence of senior combat soldiers.

"We're putting you on guard duty," I ordered, trying not to laugh.

"What do I have to do?" he asked.

I pulled my M-4 off my shoulder.

"You're in charge of securing the weapons," I told him as I placed it under his pillow.

"Okay, sir. When will you be back?"

"When we're back," I answered, as my mate placed his larger M-16 under the pillow.

We left the building before bursting into laughter and getting back to our party plans, hopeful that the cadet would be there with our weapons when we returned because there would be no reduction in jail time for coercing a kid to babysit our guns. In fact, I reckoned they'd possibly lay a few extra charges if we were ever caught for this stunt.

But we were Golani, and that's what we did.

The party went until the early morning. When we arrived back in the room at about 4am, the poor bugger was wide awake, protecting our guns for dear life.

"Thank god you're back!" he blurted out, almost uncontrollably.

A few months later, he probably laughed at himself for falling for our bluff.

While I'm sure there were many moments in the army where I pissed my comrades off, I always seemed to have the respect of those around me because, at the end of the day, I wasn't being forced to serve. I chose it.

My past wasn't a secret. People knew I had left a life of drug addiction and petty crime back in Melbourne, which ironically seemed to generate even more respect. I was only 19 or 20 years of age and had already lived more of life than most people twice my age.

The conflict between the Israelis and the Palestinians was, to me, a pretty simple one. The biggest problem for the Palestinians was their own leadership, but that was not something we could sort out. That was an issue for them. Our job was to patrol the border and protect Israelis, which we did.

As for Israel itself, I loved the country, and the so-called Jewish state wasn't at all like I had imagined. I had no idea when I arrived, that a quarter of the country was non-Jewish. My commanding officer in the army was an Arab, and a lot of my friends were Muslims. I discovered that Israel was actually one of the most multicultural and tolerant places on the planet.

Experiencing that melting pot definitely shaped some of my views on things today. We like to think of Australia as a multicultural success, yet many here are easily offended. No matter the intent, everything you say seems politically incorrect these days.

Western 'wokism' is killing the natural progression of cultural assimilation in Australia. People who identify as woke have made it their life mission to be offended by the ever-growing list of absurd things they suddenly deem politically incorrect, often on other people's behalf.

By contrast, in Israel, arguably, in Aussie terms, everyone would be considered something of a racist, and yet no one was offended. They would argue non-stop, yet no one would ever take it personally.

I remember sitting on a bus listening to two old men arguing about who was the bigger tight-ass – Yemenites or Persians. Now, of course, outside of Israel, it's always the Jews who cop that slur. But in a majority Jewish country, I guess you needed to be more specific. I learnt the stereotype was generally attributed to either Jews from Yemen or from Iran.

And watching oldies argue over it was brilliant.

"Yemenis are not tight asses; we are just frugal. Not like you Persians," one insisted.

"What? Persians are smart with their money! Not like you Yemenis," the other countered.

Back and forth it went, much to the amusement of everyone on the bus.

It was the most racist argument you could imagine. And it was totally fine. That's just the way people talked in Israel, and no one blinked an eye or made a big fuss about it.

In a weird way, Israelis are more racist, yet at the same time more tolerant than Australians, certainly more than 'woke' Australians.

Native Israelis are referred to as Sabras, alluding to a persistent, thorny desert plant, known in English as prickly pear, with a thick skin that conceals a sweet, softer interior.

They are blunt and to the point, but they have had to be. There is little time for pleasantries when the very existence of your nation is, and always has been, under threat.

I laugh at idiots in Australia protesting so-called existential threats like global warming and climate change or whatever the kids are calling it these days. Go live in Israel, surrounded by hostile nations that want to destroy you, and then you'll know what a real existential threat looks and feels like.

CHAPTER FIVE

FINDING MY VOICE

Sarah and I had an intense long-distance relationship throughout the second half of my military service.

Phone calls with loved ones could only be taken in very short, designated breaks for everyone else, but not me. She and I were always on the phone discussing and planning the dreams of our future life together. Command overlooked my daily hours of Sarah talk time because I was an exception to the strict base phone use rules.

"Where's Avi?" I often heard people requesting in the background, followed by, "he's talking to his Sarah." Pronouncing her name with a thick Israeli accent emphasising the 'ch' in the back of the throat.

"Oh, of course. His new wife S-a-chr-a!" the others would chuckle in response.

Soldiers and commanding officers felt a bit sorry for me. We were doing seventeen days on and four days off.

On the days off, my fellow soldiers would go to their parent's home's to receive loving embraces and home-cooked meals. I'd just go to my apartment and talk to Sarah.

Unlike the first half of my service, bars and girls were no longer how I spent my time off deployment.

So, on base, there were no restrictions on me talking to her. I had a free pass unless, for obvious reasons we went into Gaza on a mission.

Our main job, when we were there, was to patrol the border. Usually, in a convoy of three vehicles, we'd drive up and down the fence line to ensure no one is trying to get across the border.

Shifts were four hours; you usually got one or a maximum of two shifts and then a four-hour break before another shift. Describing us as tired would have been an understatement. We were mainly running on autopilot.

Usually, the driver and sergeant sitting up front were the only two personnel awake in each vehicle. Everyone else would be woken up if and when something kicked off. I was always awake though, talking to Sarah.

One day, we were on patrol in a convoy of two Jeeps leading the way, followed by a truck. I was alone in the back of the specialised military truck, which had two benches along each wall that could seat up to five combat soldiers in full gear on both sides. In between the benches, there was decent sized empty floor space.

Jeeps and Hummers used on patrol were much more comfortable to sit in for the four hours shifts, which is why most soldiers opted to ride in them.

Not me.

I saw the unique opportunity the truck presented with all that wasted space. Obviously, I wasn't willing to sit on those uncomfortable benches. After ten minutes, sitting on those things would break my back, let alone four hours.

No, my plan was grander. I created a bed fit for a king on the floor between the benches using a bunch of soft sleeping bags I borrowed from the barracks.

I lay down, stretched my legs comfortably, and, of course, talked to Sarah through the earphones plugged into my head, being perfectly propped up by a pillow I'd also commandeered from the sleeping quarters before the shift.

As we were talking, she questioned if everything was okay.

"Why?" I asked.

"I think I can hear gunshots," she answered nervously.

"Oh crap, you're right!" I screamed as I jumped up and dropped the phone.

The sound of slugs hitting the bulletproof truck was loud and clear now. And just like that, my beautifully designed safe space was no longer.

Sticking my head out the back, I saw my comrades-in-arms leaping from the Jeeps and taking cover behind sand dunes as shells hit the ground all around us.

The leading vehicles had been parked perfectly to allow their evacuation.

Drivers were trained to park at 45-degree angles so the fighters could exit using the cover of the bulletproof vehicles and engage the enemies.

Unfortunately, my driver didn't. It looked like he'd pooped himself and ran before making it safe for me to get out.

There was no way in hell I was jumping out. I had zero protection. I could see the bullets hitting the ground I would have to jump onto. The truck still felt safer than what was going on out there.

That was until there was a massive explosion ten or fifteen meters away. The terrorists began firing rocket-propelled grenades at the truck. I was now stuck between a rock and a hard place, or more accurately, bullets and a truck about to blow.

With no choice, I had to get out.

It was time to put all my Rambo inspiration into use. I leapt from the truck as if my life depended on it. Because it did.

I somehow landed flawlessly positioned to commander crawl perfectly to towards a sand dune for cover. Thank you Rambo.

And thank God, this time, my gun didn't jam.

I pointed my M4 in the direction the shots were coming from, and kept firing, stopping only to change magazines, which I did five times. Meaning I fired almost 100 rounds at those bastards who ruined my quiet, comfortable conversation with Sarah.

Then boom. A targeted Israeli missile exploded on the other side of the border, and the attack was over.

I got back into the truck, and I could see that Sarah was still on the line.

"Hey, all good," I reassured her as I picked the phone up.

"Oh my God, that was so scary," she exclaimed.

It was. For both of us.

At the debrief of the incident, where every moment of the ambush was investigated and unpacked, my DIY, cosy little bed arrangement was exposed.

It turned out the only part of the truck that wasn't bulletproof was the floor between the seats. Exactly where I lay.

While we certainly eliminated the terrorists that day, they didn't leave empty-handed. They destroyed my safe space. The bed was now banned.

A month later, Sarah came to visit me in Israel.

Pursuing a long-distance relationship while serving on the frontline in Gaza was tough enough. Making it even more challenging were the insane phone bills that neither of us could afford. Do you remember the days before Facetime? We'd pay per minute just to talk, for hours on end, often about nothing.

The phone bills got so crazy that, after a few months apart, we figured it was probably cheaper for her to visit.

My commander approved a two-week holiday to spend with her travelling the country, on one condition: I bring the famous S-a-chr-a to the base to say hi.

Yes, sir. Deal.

Some of my closest cousins, Yael and Merav, who were living in the Yemini family neighbourhood in Kfar Sabba, helped me plan for Sarah's arrival.

Merav took me to a jeweller in Bnei Barak, an ultra-orthodox city neighbouring Tel Aviv, where I could purchase an engagement ring at an affordable price.

Back then, the average Israeli Army salary for conscripts was approximately a thousand Aussie dollars a month. Mine was about double plus accommodation, as I was considered a 'lone soldier'.

I saved up for a few months ahead of Sarah's arrival.

Merav helped me pick a ring that cost almost a month's pay. I booked a fancy restaurant on the top floor of the Azrieli Mall in Modiin.

Yael drove me to the airport to pick Sarah up. I was nervous but excited.

I'll never forget waiting at the gate for Sarah as she arrived in Israel, not because it was romantic but because the weight of it all hit me.

On the one hand, I was eager to see the woman I had grown to love from the daily conversations dreaming about what life could be together.

But at that gate, I also realised I was just a 20-year-old kid, spending hours on the phone each day talking to an older woman a world away who kept telling me how badly she had suffered at the hands of another man.

It felt good to give her comfort over the phone. But now, she was about to be here. And the reality of it suddenly terrified me.

Standing at the gate waiting for her to come out the big doors, Yael and I were bantering. I was trying my best to mask the worst case of nervous butterflies from my excitement mixed with the gut feeling that this was wrong.

As soon as I saw Sarah walk out, rolling a trolly with her suitcase on it, the feeling I was making the biggest mistake of my life got even more intense. Unbeknownst to Sarah, I was fighting an internal battle as she walked towards me.

Sarah wasn't just much older than me. She was a mother who had travelled across the world to see me. I know this is going to sound awful, but I was like, "shit, am I really doing this?"

My brain was telling me to put a merciful end to this. But my heart was guilting me, pointing out how I saved her from that other mean guy and how she's come all this way to be together.

I couldn't possibly end it now.

When my brain realised my soft soul was going to win, he started justifying the bad decision for me.

"You did buy an expensive ring and plan a romantic proposal," my mind said. "It would be a massive waste not to use it now."

We visited the base as I promised my commander. We even got a photo in front of the famous truck. The scars on the vehicle from that day were evident, which we thought would one day be a cool story to tell the kids.

The day I proposed, I barely ate. Not because of nerves. I'd come to terms with my immature decision. Gosh, I wish I could go back and talk some sense into that young 20-year-old fool.

I barely ate that day because I knew dining at the lavish restaurant was going to cost a packet. I wanted to get my army-salary money's worth.

Waiters welcomed us, showing us to our table. There were probably less than twenty others dining in the restaurant. Everyone looked pretty dressed up and classy. And then there was me, in my army greens.

I excused myself to the bathroom so I could sneak the ring to a waiter.

"Please bring this out with her dessert," I instructed.

"Okay," the young lady said with excitement.

It was the kind of place that likely had a wedding proposal every second day. But the Aussie-soldier factor seemed special for her.

I was starving and couldn't wait to dig in.

Sitting back down, we both placed our orders. No entrees, just mains. This was no time for a snack.

Sipping on wine and making small talk, we waited for food.

A waiter finally came out with our dishes, and I almost lost my mind. He had placed this massive plate in front of me consisting of a tiny piece of foreign-looking stuff set faultlessly in the middle.

I'm sure Sarah could see the horror in my eyes as I placed the weird little meat salad thing in my mouth. By the time I was done swallowing, Sarah was just about finished her costly slice of celery or whatever that was.

"Dessert please," I ordered with my hand up.

A few minutes later, the young lady I spoke to earlier came out with another waiter. He was holding our dessert, and she was carrying the ring.

I'm not sure why I don't clearly remember what happened next. She obviously said yes. I think she knew what was going on as soon as we walked in. Why else would we go somewhere so fancy? Especially because neither of us could afford it.

The next thing I recalled was rushing downstairs to eat pancakes in the mall because I was still so freaking hungry!

The highlight of Sarah's trip was done. We were engaged to be married, and so back home to Australia she went.

After she left for Melbourne, I was eager to return to the army when my special leave to spend time with her expired. In hindsight, my enthusiasm at returning to the unit should have been a big red flag that marrying her was coming from the wrong place. But like I said, I was 20 and so naive.

As my service drew close to an end, Sarah and I started to plan what we would do when I returned home.

My skills were quite specific, and there were not many obvious career paths for uneducated ex-Israeli soldiers with banged-up bodies.

Throughout my service, I maintained my physio exercises to stop my shoulder surgery from reversing.

Before the reconstruction, my shoulder would dislocate if I sneezed wrong. I'm not joking. One time I was on a train in Melbourne with my left arm out, and I sneezed. Pop. My shoulder was hanging from the joint. By that point, it was such a regular occurrence I had learnt to put it back in myself. As painful as it was, there was no way I was going to wait hours at a hospital for a doctor to do it for me.

The first time it popped out was when I was mucking around at Elsternwick station as a young teen. I had no idea what had happened, just that I couldn't move my arm. It was hanging from the socket.

There was a group of six of us, three boys and three girls.

They all thought I was just joking. I guess (nervous) laughing wasn't helping me. I was in severe pain.

A minute or so into the ordeal, one of the girls said, "I think this is real".

"It is, I swear!" I said with a more serious face.

While the others remained unconvinced, she called me an ambulance using the payphone at the station.

Paramedics arrived fifteen minutes later, feeding me a green whistle that quashed the pain. For a minute at least.

The rest of our group finally believed my 'hanging arm' wasn't a prank when the ambulance asked which friend was accompanying me to the hospital to have my shoulder put back in.

Waiting in the ED for hours until a doctor finally came around and popped it back in with one swift movement was worse than the initial injury.

After successful surgery, I thought it would simply return to normal. Boy, was I in for a surprise. Physios gave me a rehabilitation program that I was supposed to commit to indefinitely.

I didn't. A month after quitting the recommended exercises, my shoulder suffered a subluxation.

It was the warning I needed. A complete dislocation would have caused serious irreparable damage to the surgery.

I did not want to end up there.

I became strict about doing my physio exercises. So strict that during advance training, when we got even a half-hour of downtime, while every soldier fell asleep in his place, I would be there with my elastic band tied to a tree doing my shoulder exercises.

It was difficult at times, but it's what got me into a routine of exercising.

While deployed on the Gaza border, I began adding other bodyweight exercises to my daily physio training.

I got to a point where I did hundreds of pushups and chin-ups every day, and my consistency motivated others to join me.

When brainstorming about what I might do when I return to Australia, Sarah suggested personal training. I thought it was a great idea and made obvious sense.

I was essentially doing it for free for the boys on base.

Sarah signed me up to do a course with The Australian Institute of Fitness, which was set to start a few weeks after I landed back home.

Before leaving Israel, I had one thing I needed the army to do for me. The rod and pins in my ankle from the pre-army surgery were killing me in the winter due to the cold. I wasn't sure when I'd be able to pay for surgery to remove them, so I wanted to take advantage of the military's medical cover.

I went to see the brigade doctor, who was very surprised to hear about the metal in my ankle.

"I don't see anything in your file," he questioned.

"Um, I kinda hid it, or I wasn't going to have a high enough medical profile score to be here," I answered, unafraid of being caught since my service was ending anyway.

He laughed. "Good on you, soldier."

"I'm going to look you up when I visit Australia, and you'll show me around after I approve this operation," he added, smirking as he signed off on my surgery.

About a month later, I was checked in at the Meir Hospital in Kfar Saba, in the same city my extended family lived. It was about two weeks before Christmas, and they told me we had to wait for an available surgical theatre as my case wasn't a priority.

The hospital was full of Arab patients and their massive families visiting. But that didn't stop me from walking around and making friends as I waited for my turn.

After a week, I was getting restless and was sick of hanging out with everyone else's families. I began pressuring anyone willing to listen in the hope they could get me into surgery.

I even hit up my great uncle, Yael's dad, who was head of the radiology department. Which seemed to work.

A day or so later, the surgeon came to see me.

"Avi, I can give you two options," he began.

"You can go into surgery today, but it'll be done under local anaesthetic. Or you can wait until a spot opens, likely in the New Year."

"Will I feel it if we do it today under local anaesthetic?" I asked.

"Not pain. You'll be awake and feel some light fiddling around, but it won't hurt, and you won't see what we're doing," he promised.

"Let's do it," I answered in excitement.

Confidently lying in the theatre as they injected the local anaesthetic. I was oblivious to the world of pain I was about to enter.

"No pain!" the surgeon had promised. Do you know what it actually felt like? It felt like someone was unscrewing four bolts and removing a rod from my bone.

The only thing I didn't feel was the skin being cut.

Recently, when I told a surgeon in Australia that story, he laughed and said, "local anaesthetic doesn't work on anything below the flesh".

Where was he when I needed that information?

After recovering from that ordeal at the end of my military service, I arrived back in Australia energised to take on my Certificates III and IV course in fitness that Sarah had signed me up for.

Staying in Israel was not an option, because Sarah had split custody of her young boys, making it impossible for them to leave Australia.

It was one of many sacrifices I was willing to make to begin life with our new little family.

I finished the fitness study effortlessly enough, but an interaction on the last day of the course would forever change my thinking.

There just happened to be a Palestinian kid in the same class who took exception to me having served in the IDF.

"You know why there's never going to be peace in the Middle East?" he asked me on the last day of class.

"Why?" I asked, intrigued. Because I don't often get to hear from the other side.

"Because our Koran says so," he told me. And then he just walked off.

I hadn't read the Koran at that point in my life. The entire time I was in Israel, I had assumed that Jews were loyal to Israel because they were Jews and Arabs were dedicated to the Palestinian cause because they were Arabs. It was all about tribal and ethnic loyalty, I'd thought. And I understood that.

But this Muslim kid was telling me that his religion meant peace was impossible.

That interaction stuck in my mind. Later, when I read how the Koran and other Islamic scripture depicted Jews, I realised why peace in the Middle East, not just with the Palestinians, has historically been so challenging.

Peace in the Middle East requires much more than a few fancy words by some disconnected politicians who are thousands of kilometres from the conflict and naively assume the whole world thinks like them.

As for the Palestinian kid, I got the impression he had been waiting for the entire course to get that off his chest. He wanted me to know.

When my course ended, Sarah and I moved from Richmond to Caulfield to open my new personal training studio.

It was a shop front with a residence upstairs in a small shopping strip in the heart of Melbourne's Jewish community. We converted the front room into a reception area and the back room into a small gym.

We called it IDF Training. A play on words - Individual Diet and Fitness training with a former Israeli Defence Force combat soldier.

This was 2009, before advertising online was really a thing for small local businesses, so I spent a month delivering pamphlets all over the neighbourhood.

The problem was that people assumed an IDF soldier would train people in Krav Maga, the Israeli army's hand-to-hand combat system. They loved the idea of being trained by an ex-soldier, just not in my area of expertise. So, I decided to go where the market was.

I contracted a Krav Maga instructor from Israel to start classes in Melbourne. We rented a dance studio to try the concept close to my PT studio and had 30 people attend class on the first day. I couldn't believe it.

The classes kept growing until we had to move locations, and eventually ended up with two of the country's largest, best-equipped Krav Maga and 24/7 fitness gyms.

During this time, I changed my surname from Waks to my mother's maiden name Yemini. It was mainly to avoid confusion with everyone else in the family because whenever I sent an email signed as Waks, people often responded by asking which one I was. And I couldn't blame them. There were 17 of us, after all.

Changing my name felt right. I had always identified much more with my Yemini side of the family in Israel. I never felt like a Waks. It also helped to establish me as my own person at home in Australia, and I've never regretted it.

Running gyms would have been my life had I never sat down to watch ABC News one particular night in 2012.

You may find this difficult to believe, but in 2012, I was not political at all.

Honestly, I wouldn't have been able to tell you the difference between a conservative and a progressive or what was meant by left and right in political terms.

Don't get me wrong, I had opinions on things, but I was generally apathetic about politics.

John Howard? Kevin Rudd? Did it really matter? Australia was a relatively stable place, and there didn't seem much to be concerned about beyond the usual to-and-fro of local issues. Certainly not compared to Israel, where I had seen first-hand what it meant to live in a high conflict zone, under the constant threat of bombardment.

I would watch the news, but I never overthought what was being presented or what any of it meant. Current events were interesting but inconsequential. I had gyms to run, a wife to care for, her two children and the two young children we had together to raise.

All of that changed one night when I sat down to watch ABC news and saw a report on Israeli operations in Gaza.

For the first time that I can remember, I was genuinely annoyed by news reporting. I was watching the report and thinking to myself, "You're just manipulating facts. I've been there and seen it, and what you're saying is not the truth. It's a distortion of the truth."

In fact, it got me so riled up that I logged onto our gym's Facebook page and vented to our 50,000 followers. And then I posted again. And again. I started using the platform we had built to promote our business for broadcasting my opinions on the Israeli-Palestinian conflict.

Some people loved my posts, while other people, including some gym members, were furious. I didn't give a shit. I had a pretty simple message for those who complained about my ranting on the gym's Facebook page.

"You're coming to learn Israeli defence force training, which is based on their army's mentality, approach and style of self-defence. If you're unhappy that I'm expressing an opinion in favour of the people and method you're practising, go learn a different form of combat somewhere else."

Not surprisingly, my Facebook posts lost us some customers, but also gained others. More importantly, they stirred up a lively debate. And amidst all that, I was finding my voice taking on the official narrative.

When the war in Gaza ended, I continued airing my opinion on other things. People seemed to be interested in what I had to say, and I enjoyed the debate and, let's be honest, the limelight.

Around that time, for instance, there had been a rise in Islamic terrorism, and so I was pretty vocal about the need for police to be given greater powers to combat the threat. This was, of course, ironic considering the stand I would take ten years later when those same powers were used against citizens in Melbourne during the Covid pandemic.

As a teen, I had a bunch of Muslim friends. Then I joined the Israeli Army, and there too, I met great Muslim soldiers.

But I started to learn more about Islam when I realised something dark about the Muslim community in Australia. It was partly promoted by the Palestinian kid in my fitness course, but even more so by a guy called Mahmoud Chatila, whom I started following on Facebook because I was, as a gym owner, inspired by his story.

Mahmoud, nineteen at the time, ran from Melbourne to Sydney to raise awareness after his father died from stomach cancer.

His entire approach to everything that had happened was motivating to me. I sent him a message of support, and we chatted a little.

Fast-forward to 2014, and war was once again raging in Gaza. Mahmoud put up a pro-Palestinian post which was fine. His post wasn't radical. From memory, it had a degree of class like Mahmoud himself.

But the comments? Wow! The most vile, anti-semitic hate you've ever read. And it kept going and going. Almost every single comment called Jews, not even Israelis, just Jews: Dogs.

If the tables were turned, there'd be public outrage over "Islamophobia". But not even Mahmoud – who had obviously seen the comments - said anything.

It made me wonder if this clearly decent Muslim was okay with such vile Jew hatred. There was something deeper worth exploring.

Through the hundreds of hateful people commenting on his post, I went down a rabbit hole that demonstrated how even the Islamic community here in Australia held abhorrent views about people they didn't even know.

Until the Abraham Accords, where Trump brokered a peace deal on September 15, 2020, I had little faith in the Muslim world ever being able to see Jews as humans. Ironically, it was the man often described by the media as divisive and hateful that opened me to the idea of uniting with good Muslims. Trump's peace deal was the first time since then that I had ever witnessed online and in person such widespread genuine love from Muslims towards Jews.

The UAE is the perfect example of the solidarity between the Arab and the Jewish world. It's the only Islamic state I've been to where I can proudly display my forearm tattoo of a star of David on an Israeli flag. Locals love it.

Back in 2014, some of my gym members said they liked my take on world events, but others who loved our gym warned that it seemed inappropriate to be expressing them on a business platform.

Fair point.

So, I started an Avi Yemini Facebook page where I could just vent about whatever I wanted.

I put a message on our gym page inviting clients who wanted to hear my thoughts on anything, including world events, to come across to the Avi page, and, to my surprise, thousands did.

In 2016, still fresh on the political scene, I received the first significant backlash.

I invited Senators Pauline Hanson and Malcolm Roberts for a Q&A evening in the heart of the Jewish community.

The event sold out within hours. Right-wing Jews were excited by the idea. But self-proclaimed 'anti-fascists' announced they would travel from their far-left wing bubbles to the Jewish community on the day of the event to protest.

All hell broke loose. The Australian Federal Police came to see me in a bid to map out a plan for the senators' security.

The irony of having a group of primarily white university students who were pretending to stand for minorities by invading a minority community was astonishing to me.

One Nation ended up pulling the plug on the event, citing security concerns. For me personally, it was an introduction to the culture war I was entering.

CHAPTER SIX

GUILTY OF WANTING MY KIDS

Providing a running commentary on world issues had become a passion. Other passions of mine, however, were turning toxic.

Our gyms were successful, but I hated them. Like any small business, staffing was always a headache. Making the pain even worse was the compounding issue of huge egos that usually come with martial artists.

Krav Maga was so new in Australia that we hired lead instructors from Israel to conduct instructor courses in Melbourne merely to staff our gyms. That's how hard it got to keep up with demand.

Students felt honoured to be invited to one of these instructor courses and were always energised to start teaching. But the pattern every single time was the same.

Students-turned-instructors started out humble enough, especially when their class numbers were modest. However, their egos grew with their class numbers. Building the trainer from nothing was a double-edged sword. We needed the numbers to make the business viable. But when the numbers came, the trainer had a list of unrealistic demands, like more pay for less work, and requiring assistant staff to boost their egos.

The funny thing is you didn't need to be a particularly good trainer to get big classes. I had the sales knack so could sell just about anything to anyone. Classes grew due to clever marketing. I'd create campaigns promoting the new instructor, and the public would join his or her lesson and swear by that particular trainer.

When I didn't meet their demands, many would try to start a competing gym and quickly learnt the truth the hard way. Without my art of promotion, they failed.

On top of that aggravating reality, I felt the time I spent on the business was time I could have used to talk and write about things I was thinking about. The gyms had become a pesky distraction from political and cultural commentary.

And then there was my relationship with Sarah.

We got married as soon as I returned to Australia. Hardly a romantic experience. Just me, Sarah and two witnesses at the Victorian Marriage Registry.

Why the rush, you ask? Sarah understandably wanted a secure relationship to lock in a father for her 2 boys, aged 5 and 7 years old. They were adorable, and that made the immature decision of racing to tie the knot easier. I felt obligated to Sarah, and, if I'm honest, I didn't want to give my family the satisfaction of seeing us break up. My entire family had opposed the relationship from the start, which became a (dopey but typical) reason for me to pursue it.

I thought my family's disapproval was primarily because she wasn't Jewish, with the added (lesser) issue of already having children. In hindsight and after lengthy discussions with the most vocally opposed family members, I now realise they saw the red flags I was ignoring. Her not being Jewish was the least of their problems. In fact, even after she converted to Judaism and became more observant than many of them, Sarah was never well received. On the other hand, my now wife, who's not Jewish and never will be, is adored by my entire family. I'll tell you more about that in a minute.

The love story of Sarah and me lasted as long as our celebration.

The fighting began almost immediately. The sad reality is, like so many couples, Sarah and I were mismatched from the start. And, despite the holes in our marriage so early on, soon we were a family of six.

Our daughter arrived on a clear-skied cold July night in 2009. We barely reached the birthing centre on the other side of town before she almost fell out.

The morning my baby girl was born, I looked at her tiny pink face and wondered how anything could be so beautiful. She smelled scrumptious. I loved everything about her and everything she did. She could do no wrong, no matter how annoying a baby can get. Even her first poop had me mesmerised. Becoming a biological father for the first time was the proudest moment in my life until that point.

Her brother came along a little over a year later. His birth was a bit more problematic as he had to be placed in NICU for precautionary reasons. I sat there for a week watching various horror stories unfolding around me. I remember feeling guilty staring at my perfectly healthy-looking child surrounded by babies, some of whom would not make it and even those who would survive were destined for a life of pain. Truth be told, I knew my baby boy was going to grow up to be a bit of a troublemaker like his dad—demanding attention like that from the start. The universe gave it back to me tenfold, in the best way.

One salient reality existed for me as a father: I wanted my children to grow up seen and loved. And I wanted them to know a happy home.

But, issues in a marriage don't dissolve simply because children are in the picture. In our case, it only exacerbated the problems that were already there.

Ironically, Sarah's conversion to Judaism played a significant role in the breakdown of our relationship. I'd escaped my religious parents to marry a secular girl, only for her to embrace religion more zealously than even them.

But it wasn't just that. We fought over everything.

It was bad. Toxic. I don't blame it all on Sarah. It was both of us. We were just a complete and utter mismatch.

It's not that I wasn't attracted to her. Sarah was intelligent and articulate.

Sarah often used big words, which I admired because it was what I saw as my weakness. She'd refer to herself as a writer, which I guess was fair as that's pretty much how she spent her days.

Throughout our relationship, she authored everything on my behalf, from emails to our gym members, to confrontational messages for my family.

Sarah was the writer, not me, and this unfortunately made me feel inadequate to communicate for myself. Of course, all of this seems ironic now that, of the two of us, I'm the published author. But that only happened after years of rebuilding my confidence.

When Sarah arrived in Israel, I was a breezy kid, and she was a woman with two young children.

It's like I had gotten myself into a hole, and I didn't know how to get out of it. It was sort of expected that I would propose to her while she was in Israel, and so I did.

It took me nine years to find the courage to leave, but only for a few weeks. Our lives were so intertwined and co-dependent – the business, the kids (two from her previous relationship and two we had together) – that I begged to come back. A year after that, I ended it for good.

We sold both gyms for pennies but I was just relieved to finally be free.

I scrounged some work doing social media stuff for a fledgling political party called the Australian Liberty Alliance and ran unsuccessfully as one of their candidates at the 2018 Victorian election.

Around that time, I met Rhonda.

We'd both been single for a while and had begun testing out the new world of online dating.

Neither of us was looking for something serious. We both felt like we'd been there and done that.

But we bonded immediately. Rhonda was kind, thoughtful, loving, and caring, and I was instantly attracted to her and her personality.

Rhonda quickly showed me how good life could be in partnership with the right person. She was supportive, affectionate and loyal. Traits that were foreign to me in a relationship.

It wasn't until I met Rhonda that I realised how unhealthy my previous marriage had been.

I guess I didn't know what I wanted or expected as a 20-year-old. Heck, I didn't even know myself.

Having separated from Sarah, all I knew was that I would never be someone's psychological punching bag again.

It was now clear to me that I yearned for someone to love, but also for someone who would love me right back; someone whom I would happily do anything for, and someone who would, in turn, feel the same way about me.

And that's what I got from Rhonda straight away.

Not only was Rhonda loving and caring, but she was also an absolute trooper.

From the beginning of our relationship, we trained at the gym every day. It was clear from then that she had much more mental strength than me, constantly pushing me to go harder.

One day she wasn't feeling well and stayed home. It was odd for her. If she's not working, she's doing stuff for the kids, cleaning, cooking, but she's never just sitting around.

I just assumed it was the flu or something. She didn't complain much, just stayed in bed.

I went off to work, and a few hours later, she was hospitalised with sepsis. It turned out she'd been really sick and soldiered through it until it almost killed her.

I realised that day how tough this woman was. I'm the biggest baby when my throat hurts a little.

It had been eighteen months since my split with Sarah. We were mostly amicable, and the kids stayed with me almost half the time.

So, I didn't think much of it when I posted photographs of Rhonda and me online, celebrating the new us. I never showed Rhonda's face because my haters are horrible people, and I wanted to protect her from them. Still, I never imagined what would happen next. The toxicity of my relationship with Sarah was about to be dwarfed by the Chernobyl that was our divorce.

After spending seventy-two hours crammed on commercial flights full of sweaty and tired travellers, I finally arrived home two days before Christmas of 2018. My son's birthday is Boxing Day, so I had three days to recover. By this point, I'd been counting down the hours to see my children, give them Christmas presents - like the naughty Jew I am - and celebrate my son's special day. I was also excited to share the news with them.

My son had spent the weeks before I left for the work trip mocking me for spending so much time talking to a girl on the phone.

They hadn't met Rhonda yet.

"Are you talking to Sydney?" my son asked the first time he noticed my call taking longer than usual.

He was referring to my friend Sydney Watson whom we sometimes hung out with. He'd sensed this call was different to anything he had witnessed.

"No. It's a different friend you've never met," I answered, brushing him off.

"That's good because you'd need a ladder to kiss Sydney," he mocked, sending my daughter and I into a fit of laughter.

He had a point. Sydney is a head or two taller than me.

My long conversations with Rhonda had become the butt of most of our in-jokes up until I left. So I was more than happy to arrive home and finally introduce them to the girlfriend I had so firmly denied ever having.

But whatever excitement I had was quickly crushed. I hadn't been home ten minutes before there was an unexpected knock on the door to advise me that I would no longer be allowed to see my children.

I felt like my entire world had exploded. From that moment on, if I wanted to wish my kids goodnight, I would have to fight for it. Our relationship was frozen in time, regardless of what they, or I, wanted.

It didn't make any sense, and, honestly, it still doesn't. Did she expect me to remain single forever, or was she hoping I'd return to her? Either way, why punish our kids just to hurt me?

I was determined to fight for my children, but it was the summer holidays, and my hands were tied until the new year. Devastated, I flew to Israel to be consoled by my family, not realising worse was yet to come.

I returned home on an early morning flight, anxious yet optimistic. I hadn't spoken to my kids for three weeks, but I had been busy in my despair. I was confident that reason would prevail and that I would be reunited with my children in a matter of days.

I disembarked the plane and rushed through immigration only to be told my bags needed to be "randomly searched" by customs. It was odd, but I didn't think much of it.

The customs officer seemed nice enough, yet a little slow at her job.

I bantered with the lady, trying to hide my impatience as she slowly inspected my bags. All I wanted was to head outside for a much-needed hug from Rhonda, who'd let me know she was already there to collect me.

However, it became clear that the impossibly slow bag search was a stalling tactic when five Australian Federal Police officers suddenly appeared. They strode up to the counter where my bags were laid open. My heart sunk. I was told I was under arrest for allegations of domestic violence. The officers escorted me out of the airport and whisked me straight to an interview room in a nearby Australian Federal Police station.

Shocked, tired, and with Rhonda still waiting outside to pick me up, I trusted advice from the first lawyer who answered my frantic calls: If I was sure I'd done nothing wrong, there was no harm in cooperating. Well, I was absolutely sure that I had done nothing wrong. But I should have said nothing, regardless.

Police interviews are designed to find something to "use against you in a court of law". The officers weren't there to "get my side of the story". Their mission was to get me to admit guilt.

Exercising my right to remain silent would have been the right move, and even more so, considering I had just stumbled off a long-haul flight I was in no state of mind to be interviewed by police. I should have said nothing. Instead, I tried to cooperate and, with the twisting of details, ultimately helped write the narrative that police would use to prosecute me.

Let me be clear, I never threw a chopping board at Sarah. I did slam a chopping board on a table in frustration two years earlier. I certainly didn't throw it, let alone at her.

I would have fought the charges no matter how long it took. But here's the clincher; if I'd contested the charges, I would have had to accept not seeing my kids while there was an open domestic violence matter afoot.

Due to Australian law, when it comes to these issues, I can't publish many of the specifics, but I was left with two options on how to close the domestic violence case and see my kids:

1. Fight the charges, for as long as the process would take to clear my name, and then fight to see my kids.

2. Plead guilty to throwing a chopping board during a heated argument that accidentally hit her and be allowed to see my kids immediately.

I couldn't bear going a year or likely more without having a relationship with my children, so, I pleaded guilty to the summary assault. I chose my children over my pride. And I would do it again. Because they matter to me far more than anything in this world.

There's a day Rhonda and I call "the day we don't talk about," which was the day after being charged with the bogus domestic violence offence. We don't talk about it because I wouldn't be here today if Rhonda had not been there. I spent that day on the floor crying my heart out, distraught at the prospect of never seeing my children ever again.

Rhonda was the one person who made me feel like everything would be okay, eventually.

The fact that our society allows children to be used as pawns by vindictive ex-partners is an atrocity. I think it explains, in part, the male suicide rate. On average, 45 Australian men take their own lives each week. Suicide is the leading cause of death of young men across our country, and my bet is that a high percentage are going through similar injustices to those I experienced. I was "lucky" in that I had the resources to fight for my kids and the support to get me through what were some incredibly dark times. Many men do not.

While the assault charge was bogus, the "using a carriage service to harass" charge for sending three not-very-nice text messages to my then-wife a few years earlier was legitimate. We were married for ten years. If we started sifting through couples' phones, reading text messages, we'd likely find all sorts of unsavoury messages sent in the heat of the moment. I don't think I'm unique in that regard.

Don't get me wrong, they weren't threats. They were mean and rude. In fact, if I'd said the same things to her face rather than texting them, no "crime" would have been committed. It was the act of sending it by text message that gave police the ability to charge me with a federal offence.

I was fined $1600 for the fake chopping board incident, and a bit less for the texts.

I've paid an enormous price for pleading guilty to those charges. I've been vilified in the media, and my critics don't hesitate to falsely label me a woman basher.

I've never hit a woman in my life, let alone my ex-wife. There's almost nothing I despise more than a man who lays a hand on a woman. So, I won't pretend that the slur didn't hurt, because it still does.

But, if I had to do it all over again, I'd make the same decision. I would plead guilty to something I didn't do in order to see my children. And, as any decent parent knows, you'd pay whatever price to be with your kids.

I'm pretty much resigned these days to people calling me whatever they want. It's an old tactic that when you can't argue the issues, you instead target the person. And my detractors do it continually.

Before my haters had the "woman-basher" slur, they called me a Nazi. That, at least, I could laugh off.

My now wife, Rhonda, and my children know who I am, and that's all that really matters.

And how thankful I am that I went through it all with Rhonda by my side. Not only because it helped me pull through, but because she got to witness the truth.

As part of the process, I had to print my entire communications with Sarah from the beginning.

You know how I told you Sarah was a writer? She wrote a lot to me over the years. And Rhonda read it all, not just the three out-of-context texts that police ran with.

CHAPTER SEVEN

AVI THE POLITICIAN

I met Tommy Robinson when I was working with the Australian Liberty Alliance in 2017.

The ALA recognised my talent for promotion and wanted me to help promote their brand in the lead-up to the 2018 election. They had seen what I managed to do with my IDF gyms, watched the political commentary on my Facebook page grow to reach tens of thousands of people, and wanted in on that action.

Debbie, ALA's president, was one of the most committed-to-the-cause people I have ever met.

She put her money where her mouth was – personally funding most of the ALA's activities while courageously hitting the streets to fight for the cause.

She would attend anti-Israel rallies full of Jew-hating Jihadis to stand against terrorism without an ounce of fear. Not even the staunchest Zionists from Caulfield had the guts to do what Debbie was doing.

Debbie and I travelled the country over a weekend, holding rallies in all capital cities calling on the UK government to free Tommy Robinson from jail.

Tommy had been locked up for identifying gang members that were on trial for sexual assault of underage girls. He confronted the grooming gang members as they entered the court, reading their names to his enormous online following.

A suppression order meant Tommy shouldn't have filmed them or read their names, even though the BBC had previously done so.

Tens of thousands of people witnessed live as police arrested the activist for breaching the judge's bizarre suppression order.

The gang were subsequently convicted for their horrific crimes as Tommy sat in jail for contempt of court without the fair trial afforded to the rapists.

Locking Tommy up, live in front of the world for what many perceived as a politically motivated assault on the truth, activated millions of people globally, including some here in Australia.

As Debbie and I arrived from each airport to attend protests across the country, large "Free Tommy" crowds could be heard from kilometres away, chanting, "Oh Tommy, Tommy. Tommy, Tommy, Tommy, Tommy Robinson". In Sydney, one protester even sponsored "Free Tommy" skywriting above the Opera House.

The atmosphere at these protests for a bloke in jail on the other side of the world was electric. Aussies across the once penal colony were sending a warning back to Britain, "not this convict".

Taking their message, we then flew to England to join tens of thousands at the biggest Tommy Robinson rally worldwide as the activist sat in solitary confinement.

Australian protests for Tommy may have been large, but London, England, on the 14th of July, 2018, was something else. It made Australian protests seem insignificant. It's hard to say how many people were there, tens of thousands at least, possibly more. The streets of the capital of the United Kingdom were packed.

And when the crowd chanted his name, you could feel it vibrating back off the old English buildings.

Walking through the crowds, almost everyone stopped and thanked us for the "Free Tommy" protests back home. They were genuinely grateful for the international support for their hero.

Even getting a meal was challenging. The pubs were packed due to the sheer number of people in town. And Tommy fans certainly loved a pint or two.

It was getting late, and I was starving. I'd walked past most pubs because they looked too busy. I headed closer to my hotel, hoping to find somewhere with some space. It didn't matter how far I went; they were all bursting at the seams.

Biting the bullet, I walked into the pub closest to my hotel.

As I entered, I heard someone scream "Avi!"

I couldn't really tell who it was. After all, ninety-nine per cent of the room was taller than me. That didn't matter because most of the pub was now looking at me and cheering.

Without warning, the crowd burst into the Tommy chant, only changing it from "Oh Tommy, Tommy..." to "Oh Avi, Avi. Avi, Avi, Avi Yemini".

The attention-seeking part of me was revelling in this moment, but my stomach was dying for some much-needed pub grub.

As if reading my mind, a massive Irish bloke signalled me to get to the bar. A challenge that seemed almost impossible as the room was packed like sardines. Witnessing my struggle, he pushed his way through the still-chanting crowd to physically bring me to the front of the line.

I ordered a steak and beer, and before I could pull out my wallet to pay, someone had settled the bill.

These folk were far from rich, just grateful for our work. I can't tell you how many beers I drank that night, all I know is I got very drunk, and they didn't let me pay for a single one.

After my first trip with Debbie, Rebel News invited me to join an international team of citizen journalists to cover Tommy's trial fairly, as the British legacy media were lying or distorting the truth every step of the way.

Tommy was campaigning against the rise of Islamism in the UK and trying to alert people to the dangers of extremism. He was instrumental in shedding light on the nationwide epidemic of Pakistani (they call them Asian) grooming gangs targeting young white English girls. Of course, the media labelled *him* as the extremist and made *him* out to be the danger to a civil society.

That was my early introduction to working with Rebel as a freelancer.

Tommy was freed from prison nine weeks into his 13-month sentence after the Court of Appeal quashed the finding of contempt made against him.

Protesters globally celebrated the win, feeling vindicated they were standing for justice.

That's when I met Tommy Robinson in person.

I couldn't believe he was as tiny as me (possibly even smaller). He had an infectious smile and was full of banter. It was as if he hadn't just been to hell and back.

Even before meeting Tommy, I liked him, because I had seen first-hand the radical elements within Islam that were so dangerous to the West and was relieved to find someone else brave enough to speak publicly about it.

But, if I'm being honest, I also liked him because I saw that he had some qualities I aspired to. He was bold, brash, and crazy-brave in the face of relentless opposition. Not only did he not care what people said, but the attacks against him also seemed to drive him on. I admired that determination.

In the UK, I documented how even the Australian media reported on Tommy Robinson and his undoubtedly broad support. I'll never forget confronting ABC and SBS journalists at a "Free Tommy" rally and asking whether they were going to label Robinson and his supporters in their news reports as "far right" and "fascist" and "controversial".

The reporters hated me asking them questions. They weren't used to being on the receiving end, and threatened to report me for harassment. I thought that was hilarious and said so. Imagine the people asking the questions threatening harassment charges against anyone who dared to question them.

Those videos went viral.

By this stage of my life, having watched the way the mainstream media reported news from Israel, I was highly sceptical of journalists. They would label people and, in so doing, slant the way people received the message.

I mean, if you introduced someone like Tommy Robinson as a 'far-right extremist', then even if you went on to report what he actually said, you had already tipped the scales of public opinion against him. I didn't think that was fair. The media would use the same sly tactics when reporting news from Israel. Oh, and now they use the same tactics against me.

By calling out the media's labelling of Robinson, I made myself a target of their smear campaign. I was called everything under the sun, including, hilariously, a Nazi.

Can you imagine how absurd it is to be calling a Kippah-wearing Jew, who had spent three years fighting with the IDF in defence of the Jewish state, a Nazi? If I'm a Nazi, then I'm the most incompetent Nazi of all time!

I began wearing the Kippah (religious skullcap) everywhere and describing myself as Australia's proudest Jew just to expose the stupidity of my detractors.

Unlike Christianity or Islam, Judaism is a religion and a people. There are only 15 million of us in the entire world. There are probably ten religions in India with more subscribers. So I am really proud to be a part of one of the smallest minorities on the planet.

The only people who got upset with me for wearing the Kippah were far-left anti-Israel self-hating Jews. They accused me of using the Kippah as a prop, pointing out that I wasn't even religious.

Funnily enough, the practising Jews didn't have a problem at all. They supported me wearing the Kippah because the intent was irrelevant to them.

According to Jewish law, a man over 13 shouldn't walk more than four steps without it. So even if I was using it for a prop, they didn't care.

Plus, most of them shared my politics. They're conservatives, after all. And they loved watching a proud Jew, wearing a Kippah, standing up for what they also believed.

Tommy told me not to worry about the names or labels people put on me.

"As long as you are not what they call you, it doesn't matter what they call you," he said.

"They call me a Nazi thug. Bruv, I'm the only guy who's ever been arrested for punching an actual neo-Nazi. I saw him waving a swastika in the crowd as I was giving a speech on the stage. I asked him to fuck off in front of everyone, but he wouldn't. So I jumped off the stage and knocked him out. I hate Nazis."

"So fuck what they call you, bruv", he told me.

It was good advice, and I've had many occasions to reflect on it.

Seeing the electricity around Tommy Robinson boosted my desire to participate in politics. In the winter of 2018, I ran at the Victorian legislature with the ALA's endorsement.

The ALA endorsed me as their candidate at the 2018 Victorian election in a seat that we didn't have any chance of winning on paper.

But that didn't stop me from deluding myself that winning was possible.

I was an enemy of the state when it came to politics. The progressives hated me, and the conservatives thought I was too crazy for their side. I was saying things that many people were thinking but were too afraid to say. In hindsight, I probably could have been more measured in how I spread my message. Still, you must remember I was learning the whole political commentary gig as I went.

My work covering anti-Islamification rallies attracted the attention of a Liberal candidate running in the Victorian election. She contacted ALA after she and her daughters, who ran a local restaurant, were threatened by Muslim youths.

She told me the young men had called her daughter "a dirty white whore", threatened to rape her, and then assaulted her as she walked to her car one night, punching her in the face.

She wanted me to tell her story as a way of getting people to consider limits on immigration because multiculturalism clearly wasn't working. I was impressed. Here was a Liberal candidate courageous enough to talk about an issue that most people acknowledged privately but in public, avoided at all costs

After several meetings, she agreed to be interviewed. The problem was that when she spoke on camera, she avoided any mention of the attackers' ethnic background.

Rather than specify who attacked her daughter, as she did up until the camera started rolling, she just mentioned "two young men". Well, I thought that was pretty unhelpful because the issue wasn't the fact that they were young men. The problem, according to her, for weeks before filming was a particular ideology.

I've never liked cowards. But two-faced cowards were even worse.

I knew what she was saying. She knew what she was saying. But I needed the viewer to understand what she was saying.

So, I decided to edit the video, so people knew exactly what she was talking about. I played the Islamic call to prayer in the background when she spoke about being attacked.

"Subtle, but effective," I thought. Certainly not what I'd do today.

Later on, in the interview, she told me: "I think there are people in this country who are not coming here to get the best out of the country and to give the best that they can. I think we need to look at immigration overall."

Now I knew who she was alluding to, as she'd wasted plenty of my time telling me about it, hoping I would come to film. But on camera, she suddenly changed her tune and was deliberately vague, like any other run-of-the-mill politician.

So, when I edited the video, I felt justified in clarifying what she was saying. I wouldn't do it today because I think it's shonky journalism, but then again, I've learnt to sniff these users and abusers out before we get anywhere near editing.

Well, the shit hit the fan. Within an hour of the video being published on social media, I was getting frantic calls. "You've got to take it down!" her family began demanding - most of whom were there during many of our meetings.

The desperate candidate told mainstream media journalists she didn't know who I was when she did the interview and that she had never meant "Muslims", and certainly was not calling for a ban on Islamic immigration into the country.

At first, I was pissed off. She'd wasted so much of my time at meetings, filming, editing and producing this video. Clearly, she was just using me for publicity. It was the advertising her own party refused to provide.

The Liberal Party disendorsed her because of the video, but it was too late. She was already on the Liberal Party's 'How to Vote' cards, and ballot papers had already been printed with her name.

In the end, I just thought the whole thing was pretty funny. What a pack of idiots, all of them. From the Liberal Party leader who dumped her, to the candidate herself - none of them had any backbone at all.

I, on the other hand, was full of confidence and probably a little bit too wild. You have to remember, I had gone from a drug-addicted teenager on the streets of Melbourne, to a soldier in the Israeli army, to the husband of a woman with two kids, and then with two more of our own… and all by the time I was in my mid-twenties.

When Sarah and I broke up, I felt like I had gotten out of jail and, for the first time in my life, I was finding who I was. But I also had a pretty large online following at a time when, unlike today, you could say anything you wanted.

Looking back, I do wish I had framed some things differently. But that's the thing about life - you can't undo yesterday's mistakes. You can only learn your lessons and try to do better today.

I mainly got orthodox Jewish votes in the 2018 election, but nothing like the number of votes needed to be elected to Parliament.

It was a reality check to my ego, for sure. I walked away thinking, "Maybe I'm not as popular in the community as I am in my own head!"

CHAPTER EIGHT

AVI THE LAWYER

The Australian Liberty Alliance party never recovered from the election loss. I recovered, but barely. My ego certainly took a pounding.

The brief foray into politics hadn't been enjoyable. I'd been pulled in too many directions and hated the idea of having to do the people-pleasing thing to get their votes.

My campaign, if you can call it that, consisted of me going live on social media from outside early voting centres and trolling the major party candidates.

The first few days, Labor candidates and volunteers wanted nothing to do with me, running away from my camera phone. But by election day, they were replying to my cheeky banter in kind. I had taught them that we could have opposing views and still have a laugh. It was as if they learnt I wasn't actually the monster they've constantly been told I am.

But a Greens candidate named Dinesh wasn't impressed. Walking up to him on day one with a camera, Dinesh ran into the polling centre to complain to the Victorian Electoral Commission (VEC). When he realised I wasn't actually doing anything wrong, he sheepishly came back out.

Frustrated with my line of questioning regarding two Greens candidates being dropped - one for rape allegations, the other for producing pro-rape rap songs - Dinesh lashed out and called me a Nazi.

"Did you just call me a Nazi?" I asked in absolute shock, "I'm a Jew!"

Dinesh ignored me, but when several Jews in the line questioned his use of the term, Dinesh responded:

"He calls himself a Nazi," trying to justify his slur to the public.

Dinesh was referring to comments I made at a rally a year or so earlier that had been taken entirely out of context and then widely shared by far-left-wing groups to discredit me.

The video came from a speech I gave during which I told a large protest crowd, "Forget what names they (Antifa) call you", and then, turning to the self-proclaimed Anti-fascist mob counter-protesting behind me, I showed the Kippah on my head and said tongue-in-cheek - "I am the world's proudest Jewish Nazi".

I was mocking the Left for calling me a Nazi, when I was, and always will be, a proud Jew.

Dinesh and his friends on the Left had cut that first line and pretended not to know what I was saying.

The early voters weren't having any of it, and forced Dinesh to retreat back into the Early Voting Centre, from where he called the police.

Police arrived, only to tell Dinesh that I wasn't doing anything illegal.

Throughout that week, I continued to troll Dinesh at polling booths where we were both candidates.

On election day, Dinesh called the police again. This time an overzealous cop began to ask for my details which I happily gave until it got to my address.

"Let me write it for you, as we're live, and I don't want to be doxed" I told the officer.

He took the piece of paper and began, "Is it this address on…", threatening to say my address on file out loud.

"Stop! Don't say my address. Thousands are watching right now," I warned him.

"Your choice to film, mate," he mocked.

He was cocky but, despite his disdain for me, was not dumb enough to cross that line. The police officer didn't share it, and I confirmed it in writing.

However, not before a local Greens member asked in the comments of that live video feed if anyone knew my address so he could "share it with anti-fascist friends".

He wasn't kidding. I recognised him from Antifa rallies where they were protesting little Jewish me. He would march along-side mostly white, violent thugs who, at several other rallies, have physically assaulted me, Australia's proudest Jew, all in the name of 'anti-fascism', of course.

Unlike this particular coward, I wasn't willing to get others to do my dirty work. I tracked him down and went to his house armed with a camera, while carefully ensuring not to share his address.

His wife answered the door, and I politely asked if her husband was home. She slammed the door in my face, so I waited out front for the man trying to dox me to get home.

Ten minutes later, a police divvy van rolled into the street. The man who wanted to share my address suddenly appeared jogging behind the police vehicle. The brave hero who was happy to send violent thugs to my house had been hiding around the corner, waiting for the cops to escort him home.

"Everything alright, sir?," an officer asked through the car window.

"Yes. But you may want to let this bloke know it's not okay to dox people," I replied, pointing at the now puffed-out coward standing near their car.

The man began incoherently screaming nonsense as the officer replied, "No worries, let us have a chat with him".

Backup arrived, and the five officers walked the hysterical instigator back into his home.

A few minutes later, the police exited and reassured me that the man understood that threatening to publish my address online was not okay.

I left and thought both incidents with Dinesh and this man were over.

I was wrong.

Weeks later, the man who wanted to publish my address filed for an intervention order against me.

And then, months after the election was over, police laid five charges against me for my Dinesh shenanigans. They alleged stalking, using a carriage service to harass, assault and two other electoral offences that had never been prosecuted in our state's history.

Dinesh's win was short-lived when the Police Prosecutor was forced to withdraw the charges realising how embarrassing their loss would look in court.

Heck, how could I possibly be stalking another candidate by merely speaking to him at voting stations where we were both running for office?

The other charges were just as absurd.

The other guy rocked up to court with a team of lawyers for our first mention.

"Mate, just consent to the intervention order without admission now to avoid a judge imposing an order after trial," his cocky barrister demanded of me.

"I'm happy to consent as long as there's the same order in place to protect me," I offered.

They wanted me to agree not to be allowed anywhere near his home and never to mention his name online, while allowing him the freedom to post whatever he liked about me.

We're talking about a guy who used social media to try find and share my address with a group of radicals who often published how much they'd like someone to harm me.

His legal team wanted me to agree not to fight back if he did that again. There was no way - for my sake and my children's safety — that I'd settle on those terms.

"Tell your client I'm happy to agree to an order or no order. Whatever he prefers. But no matter what he chooses, it has to go both ways," I added, insisting on a level playing field.

"Good luck with that, mate," his barrister replied dismissively.

On the final day of our three-day trial, it was my turn to cross-examine "the protected persons".

I'd been preparing all night for it.

He was an academic who thought he was better, brighter and morally superior to me. I knew it would be his downfall.

"We're scheduled for a full day today, but how long do we need for today's hearing," the magistrate asked the man's confident team of lawyers.

"He has one witness to cross-examine. So no more than an hour, your honour," the barrister replied with a smug look on his face.

"I doubt that, your honour," I butted in.

When you self-represent, the magistrate and opposing legal council often ignore you as they discuss procedural matters.

It's a belittling tactic by the other side and probably a way for the court to avoid wasting time dealing with inexperience.

The court ignoring my input didn't bother me.

I cross-examined the bloke for four hours straight.

It was one of the best days of my life. Like doing street interviews, this guy was so easy to trip up on his own words. He was easier to destroy than I'd expected.

"Sir, what is Antifa?" I asked him as he faced the magistrate, refusing to even look at me.

"Antifa isn't a real thing. It's made up by the Far-Right like you," he snapped back.

His body language was oozing with disgust that he was required to answer an intellectual peasant like me.

I passed a printed copy of a Facebook photo of the man protesting with a group all carrying a large poster with "Melbourne Antifa" splashed across it.

"What does that say on the sign you're holding in this photo?" I asked.

"Melbourne Antifa", he whispered.

It was the final straw for her Honour.

"How dare you sit here and claim Antifa isn't real when it clearly is?" she scolded him as if working on my team.

By that point, the judge clearly didn't believe a word he said. She'd seen his hundreds of daily posts about me online and repeatedly snapped at him for being caught out on obvious lies.

"It's 4.30pm, and the court is supposed to close now. But I'm staying back to give the parties ten minutes to resolve it between themselves. Otherwise, I am going to reserve my judgment for a later date, which you may very well not like," the magistrate said, staring at his stunned barrister.

It was obvious I'd won. I was smiling ear to ear.

I felt like the dad in the Aussie film, The Castle. I turned to Rhonda, who was sitting a few rows back and winked with mighty pride. She shook her head ever so slightly as she put it down as if to tell me, "Stop. The judge will see".

But at that point, I wasn't afraid. I felt like the magistrate secretly admired what I had accomplished in the past four hours. It was artistic!

As we walked out of court to negotiate, the other party's legal team rushed me, begging for the offer I gave them on day one. An order by consent both ways.

I agreed. After all, he meant nothing to me. I only ever posted about that one incident that was over in my eyes.

He was the one obsessed with me.

"You're not so cocky now, are ya, mate?" I said, chuckling as the barrister walked away with his tail between his legs.

And I wasn't dreaming when I said the magistrate was impressed. The following day, I was back in court for one of my other matters that ended up getting dropped.

When I realised it was being heard by the same judge, I turned to my lawyer and told her the magistrate liked me.

"Not possible. She doesn't like anyone," my lawyer responded.

"I promise you, she likes me," I said confidently, grinning.

"You'd be a first. But even if she really does, the magistrate can't show it," my lawyer insisted.

I'm pretty good at reading people. However, my lawyer knew the magistrate and the court system much better than I did, so I dropped the subject.

My case was called. And as I walked in, lawyer by my side, the judge looked up and said cheerfully, "Oh, you again! Lovely to see you, Mr Yemini!".

"Yes, ma'am," I smiled back, before winking at my lawyer.

"I told you."

CHAPTER NINE

THE END OF THE BEGINNING

Most of my life, to that point, had been a crazy, chaotic ride. Attention to detail hadn't exactly been my forte, and everything from child support paperwork, (I'd been giving Sarah cash but had never filled out the official forms) to tax returns were in a mess.

Rhonda patiently and graciously worked through everything with me. It was a process of dusting myself off in every area of life and putting things right.

And when – after a long distressing year I was finally reunited with my two children, everything was right.

While sorting out my life, Tommy Robinson had gotten in touch, offering me the chance to work for TR News, an alternate media company he had created. He loved my way of weaving in comedy and banter to serious political and social issues. I immediately accepted his offer.

I loved working for Tommy, but it was very chaotic because he was, and still is, quite literally an enemy of the state. In fact, "Enemy of the State" was his first book title, and it was no lie.

You never knew when Tommy would be imprisoned and have all his accounts frozen. It meant that most of Tommy's team in the UK was more focused on handling crises than developing media content, so I often felt like I was a one-man team.

But having said that, Tommy was a great boss, and I still consider him a good mate.

Our lives and backgrounds could not be more different. Tommy was a soccer hooligan who became an activist and then a media proprietor, so there is no denying he had a rough side. But everything they claim about him – being racist, a thug and whatever else - is just completely false. In my opinion, he is one of the most persecuted people in the UK.

A lot of Tommy's experiences resonate with me. I was wrongly arrested three times before Victoria Police were, through court action forced to finally issue me with a grovelling apology. I know what it's like to have the authorities go after you.

I also know what it's like to have terrible things said about you, and how tiring it is to defend your reputation. I'm not saying Tommy's an angel. He isn't. I'm just saying that he's a top bloke; nothing like how he's portrayed in the media.

While they painted Tommy as a thug, I never saw him start a fight. I did witness him finish them, though. And I think the distinction is essential.

He was always getting physically attacked by people underestimating him due to his size. Tommy is small. No, actually, forget what I told you earlier, that "Tommy is possibly smaller than me". I need to get this off my chest. Tommy is tiny. A lot of people don't know that about Tommy Robinson, but I want to go on record as saying that he is even shorter than me!

Gosh, that feels better.

Seriously though, in the first week I met Tommy, he walked into a restaurant near Luton looking for something to wrap his knuckles in. He had clearly been in some sort of altercation, and his hands bore the scars.

I asked our mutual friend who walked in with him what had happened?

"Some Antifa geeza came out of nowhere and began abusing Tommy. I warned him it wasn't a good idea. But he took a swing anyway, and Tommy put him on his ass."

I had travelled around the UK with Tommy and saw first-hand how incredibly friendly he was to everyone, even people who disagreed with him.

One time we were in a mall, and a "Muslim lad", as Tommy would refer to him, walked up and asked for a photo.

"Of course, bruv," Tommy answered.

"I'm gonna post it in my Asian group for all the lads," the young Muslim man said to him.

"So let's do a video for bants," Tommy offered.

The man loved the idea, and Tommy spent ten minutes creating a funny video for this random Pakistani bloke to have fun with his friends.

I asked Tommy why he did that.

"Bruv, I like lads like that," he answered.

Tommy never judged anyone on their race or religion, no matter what the media claimed to the contrary.

He was always up for a battle of ideas with anyone. And he hated racists more than woke pretend journalists, who I guarantee had a less diverse friendship circle than Tommy Robinson.

I often went out with him, and he'd be the minority. All his friends were brown or black.

But the thing I really admire about Tommy is that he doesn't take shit from anyone.

I'll never forget the night Tommy suggested we hang out in a gay bar.

"Is there something you want to tell me, Tommy?" I teased.

"A gay bar is the one place in England the guys wanting to kill me won't ever venture into," he replied as a matter of fact. "It's just about the safest place there is."

There was no argument from me. It did seem unlikely that we would encounter any Islamic extremists in a gay bar.

I was having a good time in this bar, talking to strangers, when, in my peripheral vision I noticed that Tommy was talking to three much bigger Pakistani men.

It seemed friendly, so I didn't see any need to join him. But I kept an eye on the situation.

Tommy and the men were chatting, laughing, and even tapping glasses and saying cheers. Muslims drinking in a gay bar with drag queens, I guess, explains why Tommy Robinson's presence wasn't going to offend them.

But the energy suddenly changed. The three men towering over little Tommy began hassling him. Even from a distance, and with the dim nightclub lighting, the darkened shift in mood was clear.

Tommy remained as cool, calm and collected as you can imagine, which was impressive because, remember, Tommy is a midget.

Tommy was just speaking respectfully and quietly to these now hostile big lads. Still, they kept pushing him, trying to provoke him.

I began to walk towards Tommy as the men weren't letting up. It felt like it was about to kick off.

And it did. Tommy snapped.

He might be tiny, but he's got bigger balls than most people on this planet. He was not going to be intimidated, and he let them know.

There was a bit of push and shove before security raced in, grabbed us, and threw us out of the club.

"Listen lads," Tommy told security when we were out on the street, "I know you didn't see what happened, but if you go back and watch the security camera footage, you'll see that I didn't start anything. You can kick those guys out, or you can let them stay, I don't mind. But you need to let *us* back in."

Security didn't pay much attention until Tommy threatened to announce a rally outside the club.

"I'll force you to release the footage and publicly apologise with 10,000 protesters here", Tommy told them.

Five minutes later, the security guys returned to say sorry.

"You were right," they said. "You're welcome to come back in."

We enjoyed the rest of our night at the gay club without incident.

Tommy Robinson was one of the only people I knew who could just start live-streaming while walking down the street, and, in 20 seconds, there would be 20,000 people tuned in to watch.

That's why security took his warning seriously.

Everybody wanted more of Tommy because he was just such a big character.

Back then, the internet was the Wild West, and people, including Tommy, said things that they probably would have framed differently in the cold, hard light of day.

There's no question Tommy made mistakes. He got himself into more trouble than he needed to by saying things that his detractors could take out of context and used to have him cancelled, a bit like my "Jewish Nazi" scenario, but in repeat, over and over again.

I reckon I learnt as much from Tommy about what to do as I learnt from him about what *not* to do. I certainly learnt to tone down my behaviour and to think more about what I was saying.

I also learnt to fight back early. Tommy let the media and the authorities get away with everything. By the time he started pushing back, it was already too late. They had already utterly destroyed his reputation.

My take-zero-shit policy that you see today stemmed from a conscious decision to stop them from obliterating me as they did Tommy.

Tommy was increasingly targeted by authorities, and so while working for his organisation was exciting, it was incredibly unpredictable. He was regularly being arrested – almost always unfairly - and it started to feel like just one blow after another.

At one point, a judge jailed Tommy all over again for the same contempt case he'd already successfully appealed. It was a never-ending saga.

I felt sorry for Tommy's family. They're beautiful people. But his activism has put them through hell. His children were attacked in school, and his wife, Jenna, often found herself parenting alone while Tommy was incarcerated. While he was in jail, she would also have to manage the business.

Jenna was there for me, when I should have been there for her. But there was nothing I could do to make her life better. He was my boss, and I relied on him, (and when he was in jail, I relied on Jenna) to feed my children. But Jenna never complained. The luckiest thing Tommy had was his loyal wife.

What ended up bringing Tommy's media company down was a massive lawsuit from a Syrian refugee backed by some seriously powerful people.

"I have to shut down TR News, bruv," Tommy told me on the phone. "But don't worry, how do you feel about starting something new that's not associated with my name?" he asked.

Launching a new media company with a decent budget, not associated with his destroyed reputation, was a tempting offer. But I knew the work involved, and I wasn't sure that was the direction I wanted to go.

I loved working in front of the camera but wasn't too keen to get involved in the backend. My PTSD from running my gyms was kicking in.

I'd previously met Rebel News founder Ezra Levant on a trip to the UK in 2018 and was incredibly impressed by what he had created. I did a few gigs with him as a freelancer and later collaborated with TR News in several ventures that were super successful.

I called Ezra, explained my predicament, and asked how he'd feel about me joining Rebel News if Tommy gave me his blessing. I didn't want to go to Rebel without Tommy's endorsement. I've never used people as a stepping stone, and Tommy had always been incredibly kind to me.

Thankfully, Ezra was enthusiastic about the idea.

So I rang Tommy, and I don't think I even finished my first sentence before he told me: "You should take the job. Rebel News will be great for you. To be honest, I can't give you the support you need. Your talent is being wasted here. Fucking go there and love it."

That's the kind of guy Tommy Robinson is. My departure left a hole for him, but all he cared about was what would be best for me.

So, with Tommy's blessing, I joined Rebel News. And, just like Tommy told me, I loved it too. And I still love it.

I still have all the respect in the world for Tommy Robinson too. The critics can say what they like about him. I know him as one of the most gracious, generous people you could ever meet.

Tommy does things entirely differently from me, but his situation differs significantly from mine. They've successfully ruined him, and I cannot imagine how I'd handle his reality.

I probably wouldn't.

Tommy has been one of my greatest encouragers since the day he blessed my move to Rebel News.

CHAPTER TEN

BEATING THE FAKE NEWS

In December 2018, while I was overseas, I received a voicemail message to my Australian number, "Hey, my name's Andrew. I'm a producer at Comedy Central for The Jim Jefferies Show. Please give me a call back as soon as possible."

Interesting, I thought to myself as I hit the blue call-back button on my iPhone.

It rang twice before a chirpy voice answered, "Hey Avi, thanks for getting back to me. My name's Andrew. I work for The Jim Jefferies Show, and Jim is in Australia now filming an episode we hoped you'd feature in".

"What's the episode?" I asked.

"It's basically about the conservative political landscape in Australia, which you're a major player in", he answered, trying to stroke my ego. Which worked a little.

I hadn't followed Jim Jeffries' career closely. From what I could tell, he was a half-funny, politically incorrect comedian who had made it big in America when one of his stand-up segments mocking gun laws went viral.

The American audience gobbled up his foul-mouthed Aussie persona.

However, like many before him, Jefferies seemed to be turning his back on what had once made him slightly funny in order to fit in with the woke Hollywood crowd.

I was immediately suspicious that an invitation to feature me in a segment about Australia's right wing would be little more than a hit piece. But since when have such concerns ever stopped me? My desire to reach a new audience through the massive Comedy Central platform was too great an opportunity to miss out on.

"I'm in on two conditions," I told Andrew.

"Go ahead," he answered.

"I'll come on as long as you don't have any neo-Nazis or Nazi sympathisers in the same episode. And you have to promise not to chop and change my answers to different questions."

"Those sound like pretty reasonable requests," Andrew said, promising both would be honoured.

"Just one issue," I added.

"What's that?" Andrew asked.

"I'm not currently in Australia and I don't get back until my son's birthday in a couple of weeks," I explained.

"Hmmm. That is an issue. Let me get back to you with options," he replied, slightly disappointed.

Within a few hours, Andrew had offered to send a car to my home on January 22, 2019, to pick me up, take me to the airport, and fly me to Singapore, where Jim Jefferies would conduct the interview. He promised they'd get me a three-night hotel, all expenses paid, and return me home.

A free holiday for a 1.5hr interview which was going to feed my need for attention? I couldn't see the downside.

But with my chutzpah, I wondered if the offer could be slightly improved.

"Please book it in business class because I need sleep before landing on both ends", I told Andrew in a text message with a copy of my passport.

"I don't have the budget for business class. Is that a deal breaker?" Andrew texted back.

I bet they did have the budget, but even Andrew must have realised the deal was pretty sweet, and I was milking it for every last drop.

"Show me the schedule, and I'll confirm," I wrote back, keeping my story up while opening the door to accept his offer.

I looked at the schedule and told him I could make it work, so he was good to go ahead and book my transport and accommodation.

As promised, a car picked me up from my home in Caulfield and drove me to Melbourne Airport. I boarded my peasant cattle class flight with my chin up, knowing that I had at least tried to get the free upgrade.

Landing in Singapore, a driver was waiting to chauffeur me to the boutique hotel Andrew had booked.

As I entered the hotel lobby, a man approached, "Hey, I'm Andrew. Great to meet you finally, and welcome to Singapore!"

We sat in the lobby for half an hour discussing the state of American politics, and particularly the influence of Donald Trump. Andrew was nice enough. I could tell he was trying to make me feel comfortable about the following day's interview with Jim Jefferies.

"I'm fine as long as you stick to what we agreed, no nazis, and don't cut up my responses," I told him, just making sure he was crystal clear on the terms of the interview.

"No one else is being interviewed for this segment," he told me.

"And our editors don't engage in that type of unfair behaviour," he added, trying to assure me.

I knew he was lying, because after agreeing to come on, I went and watched a few episodes of The Jim Jefferies Show. One specifically stood out, his interview with Jordan Peterson.

It was clear to me they'd edited Peterson's interview using the unethical technique I was referring to, and yet here was Andrew claiming they didn't engage in that kind of stuff.

Smiling and nodding, I made sure not to give Andrew the impression that I didn't believe him, because I had a plan.

The next day, Comedy Central's car picked me up and took me to the interview location. It was a bar that they had temporarily re-purposed for our in-depth conversation.

I walked in, shook his hand, and made small talk as the tech team did the final touches around us.

The 5 x 5 metre room was full of staff who were so self-absorbed, they didn't notice me slip off to the side to set up two phones (in case one failed) on the couch propped up by some pillows. I was ensuring that I would have an unedited copy of our entire interview.

My heart was pounding from the excitement as I sat down without anyone realising what I'd done but then noticed one of the phones had fallen over. Shit! My plan had been so good, but now I had to reset the phone before anyone noticed.

I was prepared for a confrontation if anyone caught me. I planned to argue with them while the phones were capturing it. And if they refused to let me record my own copy of the interview, I would walk out and publish the confrontation to show the world how they tried - and failed - to stitch me up.

But I really preferred just to have the secret recording. So, back I went to reset the fallen phone, and not a single person in the room noticed.

Jim Jefferies and I talked for about an hour, sometimes we were arguing a little, but mostly just engaging in good-humoured banter that went both ways.

At the end, we took a selfie for Instagram and said our goodbyes.

I walked away, thinking maybe my suspicions had been wrong. Perhaps Jim Jefferies was actually cool, and I shouldn't have jumped to conclusions about him so quickly.

I made the most of my fully-funded holiday in Singapore by hanging out there for a couple of days before they took me home.

That was the last I heard from them until two months later.

The evening of March 20, 2019, was the Jewish holiday of Purim, where it is customary to get drunk to the point of not knowing the difference between good and evil.

I was at an event celebrating the holiday, and trying very hard to fulfil that special custom, when a rabbi walked in and said: "Wow, what Jim Jefferies did to you!"

"Huh?" I queried with a delicious 18-year-old Highland Scotch in my hand.

"The latest episode of The Jim Jefferies Show was released today. He destroyed you," the Rabbi said matter-of-factly.

"I haven't seen it. But, Rabbi, mark my words, wait until tomorrow," I promised him.

I rushed home to watch what Jim Jefferies had put out.

My original gut feeling was right. And I realised how lucky I was that I had listened to it.

Within twenty seconds of his segment, Jim Jefferies had broken the first condition of our agreement by featuring a neo-Nazi.

And throughout the episode, he repeatedly edited my answers from one question and put them to another, breaking our only other agreed condition.

Worse than breaking both our conditions, Jim Jeffries had the audacity to hold our interview and only air it in response to the horrific Christchurch massacre five days earlier.

On March 15, 2019, a white supremacist attacked a Mosque and another Islamic centre, murdering 51 innocent people in cold blood, and injuring 40 others.

The vile Australian responsible for the reprehensible mass shooting was later found to also be a rabid anti-semite.

So Jim Jeffries framed his segment with me as an effort to find out "what the people who may have radicalised him are saying".

Instead of spending the night celebrating my favourite Jewish holiday, I began working on a video that showed what Jim Jefferies had done, how he had cut and pasted my questions and answers.

For example, during our interview, Jeffries had asked me: "What gives anyone the right to tell anyone where they can and can't live?"

In his edited version, Jim cut to me, answering a different question from a very animated part of our conversation. "When you import this culture, what do you think is going to happen? Australia is going to end up the same shithole they came from that they were escaping."

Wow. I look like a radical nut.

The only problem is that my actual answer to his question, "what gives anyone the right to tell anyone where they can and can't live?" had been calmly delivered, sitting back and saying: "borders."

My secret recording shows how Jim then agreed with my answer, "I know borders, but wouldn't it be nice if we got to a place in society where we all lived as one". And I continued by saying I share his sentiment in principle, and I think most people would, but that's just not how the world works.

As promised to the Rabbi at the Purim event, I published my video exposing Jefferies' unethical edits. I showed how he broke both conditions of our interview and provided the receipts of how dishonest their editing was.

My expose blew up. Within 24 hours, it tripled Comedy Central's original video view count. It was the first time anyone had managed to flip the script on the corrupt media organisation.

As my video went viral, the comments on Jim Jefferies' video across all platforms were getting annihilated. They had successfully been exposed for their fake news. It was a beautiful thing.

But instead of removing the misleadingly edited clip from their platforms, Jim Jefferies team turned off comments and began working overtime to delete and block anyone who pointed out what they had done. Including me!

I was shocked.

First, he breached both our agreements. Then he tied me to the horrific Christchurch massacre. And when caught, rather than apologise or remove the offending material, he simply targeted anyone who dared to call him out.

I was determined not to let this go.

I crowdfunded a trip for my friend Sydney Watson and me to travel to America and confront him face-to-face.

There was no question about business class this time. Thousands of generous supporters chipped in enough for us to take the long economy flight from Melbourne to LAX.

We got off the plane and lined up at immigration separately as I was a foreigner, while Sydney, as an American citizen, had a US passport. Neither of us had any clue about what was about to happen.

As I got to the front, the immigration officer checked my passport and ordered me to wait.

Three US border agents approached and asked me to come with them. I followed to a quiet section of the airport, where they thoroughly searched my clothes, body, and bags. It felt like they were looking for something specific, but I had no idea what.

It took twenty minutes before they seemed content with their efforts, and guided me to a small room where a plain-clothed man and woman were waiting for me.

The pair introduced themselves as FBI agents, showing their identification and insisting they had a few questions.

"But before we start, I just want to inform you that California's wiretapping law requires two-party consent making it illegal to record our conversation in this state secretly," the male agent told me.

I was so confused, and my jetlag wasn't helping.

"Do you think I have a hidden camera on me?" I asked.

"We're just letting you know what the law is here, so there's no confusion," the agent answered.

I laughed.

"Mate, you guys basically stripped-searched me. What do you think I am? Mossad?"

Now that the rules were clear, the FBI agents sat me down and explained that Viacom, which is Comedy Central's parent company, had filed a complaint before I entered the country, alleging that I was a potential terrorist threat.

Can you believe these guys? First, they tried to tie me to a terrorist attack in New Zealand, and now they were telling the FBI that I was a terrorist.

After an hour of interrogation, the FBI agents cleared me. However, the process triggered a closer look at the visa waiver I had used to enter the country. They found a technicality that disqualified me, even though I'd used the same visa waiver earlier in the year to enter the United States.

When I was much younger, I had a visa application to visit my family refused because they suspected I was trying to relocate to America.

Once you've been refused any visa to the United States, you can no longer travel on a visa waiver. So they said they were turning me around and sending me home.

I spent 14 hours in the airport's detention centre with what seemed like half the population of Mexico.

It was the longest 14 hours of my life. I had no phone, there was no TV, and there was nothing to do.

When the officers finally came for me and escorted me onto a flight back home, I could not have been more excited. I didn't even care about the embarrassing long walk through the airport in handcuffs as if I was El Chapo being extradited for crimes against humanity.

As we got to the plane, they returned my carry-on luggage and personal items, so I quickly texted Sydney and told her that I was being deported.

By the time I landed back in Melbourne, my deportation had made international news. Meanwhile, Jim Jefferies and Comedy Central were copping even more flack across their social media platforms.

For months, even their most committed teams of censors couldn't stop the constant barrage of posts online pointing to what they had done in the interview and how they had resorted to calling the FBI in a desperate bid to cover it up.

But me being me, I still could not let it go. I decided to follow Jim Jefferies to a place where he couldn't have me deported. I flew to Israel, where he was planning a show for Tel Aviv.

Hours before his show was set to start, I camped out with my cameraman. We waited 100 meters or so from the backstage entrance, before security walked over to try to intimidate us into leaving.

My cover was blown, but I wasn't going to let some pesky security guard stand over me.

When he realised I wasn't going anywhere, they set up a decoy van to pretend to drop Jefferies at the main backstage area, and as I approached the van, they snuck him in the garage doors dedicated to delivery trucks.

The extent to which Jim Jefferies was willing to go in order to avoid facing me, caused another outbreak of anger online.

It got to the point where Comedy Central couldn't put out a single Jim Jefferies-related post on any platform without being ratioed.

They eventually dropped his show in November 2019, eight months after airing the edited episode with me.

On some level, I took that as a win. But I was still annoyed that he had refused to give me the satisfaction of knowing he had paid the price for finally messing with the wrong person.

That was until mid-2021 when Jim Jefferies, struggling to get a following on his sad new podcast, went on a rant about how annoying I was.

That was the glorious ending I needed to the story. Two years later, I was living rent-free in the gutless coward's head.

He doesn't have the courage to face me. Instead, he'll spend the rest of his miserable career, or what was left of it, crying to whoever would listen.

Thank you, Jimmy Boy. That's all the recompense I needed.

CHAPTER ELEVEN

RIOTS IN HONG KONG

The year before moving to Rebel News, democracy protests had broken out in Hong Kong. Tommy was still in jail, and Ezra Levant, the CEO of Rebel News had called to ask if I was interested in collaborating with Rebel News on a trip to report from the scene of the demonstrations.

At the time, I had no idea what people in Hong Kong were protesting about, let alone their history, language or culture. True, my ex-wife was half-Hongkonger, but she certainly didn't embrace it.

I agreed to go on the adventure.

I still get goosebumps thinking about those Hong Kong protests of 2019.

When I was reporting on them, I had no idea that, less than 12 months later, I'd be reporting on civil unrest in my own country. And to be honest, I've always wondered if there was a link between the two.

I arrived in Hong Kong not knowing much about what was going on. All I knew was that vast numbers of ordinary citizens were staging sit-ins to protest the government, and when you're taking on the might of the Chinese Communist Party, that's a story.

I'd covered many protests before but quickly realised this one was different. In my experience, most protesters were lefties who generally had no clue what they were really protesting about. So, you could hit them with a couple of facts – whether it's about climate change, black lives matter or whatever – and they could never give you a logical comeback. They simply didn't know their own argument.

But in Hong Kong, every protester knew the five things they demanded from the Chinese Communist Party. I was amazed at their clarity. Whatever question journalists put to the protesters, they had a response.

Their five demands were simple...

1. Complete withdrawal of the extradition bill from the legislative process

2. Retraction of the "riot" characterisation for protests

3. Release and exoneration of arrested protesters

4. Establishment of an independent commission of inquiry into police conduct and use of force during the protests

5. Resignation of Carrie Lam and the implementation of universal suffrage for Legislative Council elections and for the election of the chief executive

They weren't virtue signaling. Neither were they making vague attention-seeking arguments as are currently in vogue among protesters in the west. These Hong Kong residents were convinced that their very existence was under threat, and the Israeli side of me certainly understood where they were coming from.

The protests were spectacular. Inspiring. I could not see a way for the government to defeat them. At the largest demonstration I attended, an estimated 2 million people - out of a population of 8 million – bravely took to the streets. That's one in four citizens who were part of the protests.

They began with a sit-in at the government headquarters on March 15. Then they staged a succession of demonstrations involving hundreds of thousands of people at each protest.

As you might imagine, the government response was severe.

No one knew who I was when I first went to Hong Kong in 2019. I went with nothing but a cameraman and a burning desire to get us into the middle of whatever was happening.

I joined some Telegram groups where they'd announce pop-up protests that often grew into massive rebellions and street battles.

We jumped on a train towards the first protest and bumped into a British university professor who knew my work.

I won't name him or anyone else who helped me in Hong Kong at the time for their own safety. This particular professor happened to be very connected to the student protest movement and offered to spend the week taking me to them.

He was a godsend.

The very first protest seemed quiet at first, but as the day went on, the crowd grew in size and passion.

I walked around interviewing protesters to understand why they were there and was immediately impressed with how articulate and clear-minded they were.

Most protesters at that point were not demanding independence from China. They just wanted the "one country, two systems" status quo to be protected. They felt that the Communist Party of China was slowly but surely corrupting that agreement.

However, a small contingent also protested for Hong Kong's independence. It was easy to spot them as they waved a blue flag with "Hong Kong independence" in large white letters written in Cantonese and English. I approached one protester waving that flag who told me, "We need independence".

"What's your message for Donald Trump? Do you think he should step in?" I asked him.

Looking straight down the barrel of the camera, he begged in a thick Hong Kong accent, "Donald Trump, don't trust China! China is asshoe!"

He may not have pronounced asshole correctly, but his message and passion were easy to understand.

I didn't realise it then, but that clip would become a symbol of the protest movement after being picked up by American commentators in the following months.

It became so popular that there were viral remixes of it. My personal favourite was a Gangnam Style parody someone produced using the clip.

But the second time I had arrived that year, because of my coverage of pro-Hong Kong rallies happening in Australia, I came as a celebrity.

People supporting the Chinese Communist Party had tried to disrupt pro-democracy rallies in Melbourne that year, so I just approached them to ask which of the five demands they were against.

They couldn't tell me because they didn't even know the five demands of the pro-democracy movement. When I reviewed each of the demands with the CCP supporters, they agreed that the protester's requests were fair. And so, they looked ridiculous. And as a result, the videos became hugely popular, especially in Hong Kong and Taiwan.

I'd become a celebrity on the streets of Hong Kong and was mobbed wherever I went. The most prominent newspapers did front-page stories heralding my return.

It was insane. And I loved every second of it. It fed the attention-seeking streak that I was blessed with as a child.

Asian culture is very respectful, so it needs to be said that being mobbed in Hong Kong was the most orderly kind of mobbing you could ever imagine.

When people in Australia want to have a photo with you, they push and shove, and it all becomes quite uncomfortable. I still love it, but it gets tiring. It was totally different in Hong Kong.

One day I was covering a pop-up protest in a local shopping mall, and when it had finished, a young woman walked up and said, "you're the Australian journalist. We love you". Then asked if she could take a selfie with me.

Almost immediately, a line spontaneously formed that snaked through an entire mall. Hundreds of people organised themselves into a queue just to get a photo with me. It was the most effortless process I have ever seen. I still smile about it. They were the most polite, beautiful people on the planet.

The first trip to Hong Kong, though, was different. I didn't know anyone, and so I arrived there relying on a bit of luck to find the right contacts who could put me in the thick of the action.

Fortunately, we got chatting to that university professor on a train who knew who I was and loved what I stood for. That got us started, and from there, we met other locals and foreign independent journalists who helped us.

The second trip was a completely different story. I gained incredible access to protest organisers because everyone knew who I was, and were happy for us to be there, giving them a voice in the outside world.

I'd also hired a local videographer who spoke the language and was passionate about the cause. She was also great company, full of fun and laughter, even as her world was collapsing around her.

The nightly protests were hectic. A massive crowd would gather to peacefully chant slogans against the government before police would appear in full riot gear.

Police didn't ask questions. They would pepper spray and beat with batons whoever they could get their hands on. Then they would fire tear gas and rubber bullets indiscriminately into the crowds. I'd never witnessed anything like it before.

From what I was observing, I had no doubt the protesters would eventually have their demands met. They were just too strong in their convictions to be denied.

On my second visit, reporting from one protest, a man approached me and said hello excitedly. I assumed he was just another Hongkonger grateful for my videos challenging Chinese students in Melbourne.

"You don't recognise me, do you?" he asked with a smile.

"No! Where do I know you from?" I replied, embarrassed.

And without hesitation, he loudly proclaimed, "Donald Trump, don't trust China! China is asshoe!"

The crowd around us began clapping and cheering.

I couldn't believe it. He looked totally different.

"I made myself look a bit different, so police don't find me," he told me.

"Are you okay?" I asked, suddenly feeling guilty about the video I had made of him that had gone viral worldwide. I was worried that maybe I had ruined the guy's life.

"Yes, I'm happy. Everyone sees that video and knows the truth," he answered.

Phew!

Months later, I tracked him down again to check that he was okay and interviewed him over Skype for fans concerned about his well-being. He'd returned to his old look and embraced being a public dissident, no matter the consequences.

His bravery inspired millions, including me.

The craziest part of the daily protests was how it would be a war zone on one street, yet the next street over would be business as usual. People were shopping, eating dinner and enjoying life in a city that didn't seem to sleep.

I really grew to love Hong Kong during those trips. I hated the food. I still can't stand Chinese food, sorry. But the city and the people were terrific. I'll always be sad that I can probably never go back there for fear of being arrested and deported to mainland China.

I've often thought about returning, but it's just too dangerous. Being well-known has its downside in a communist country where the ruling party does not tolerate criticism.

The bravery of the people in Hong Kong who stood up to police brutality will live with me forever. I'd never seen protests like it.

At the time, I thought the protests were irresistible. Not only was the cause righteous, but the protesters were totally committed.

Imagine two million people - one in four Hong Kong citizens - on the streets, protesting in defiance of the might of the Chinese Communist Party. Even if the CCP rolled in with their tanks, they still wouldn't win, I thought, because most people were willing to defy the law and fight back.

Then Covid struck, and all the momentum of the protests was lost. Hong Kong suddenly slipped from the world's focus, and those of us who hadn't forgotten about the democracy movement had no way to get there to report on it, even if we'd wanted to.

The timing of Covid was interesting. Before Covid hit, the pro-democracy movement seemed unstoppable. Covid stopped it almost overnight.

While the world was distracted by the looming pandemic in their own backyards, the Chinese Communist Party took the opportunity to crack down hard on protestors, away from the glare of international attention.

And the protestors themselves were forced to put protesting on the backburner so they could focus on the seemingly more immediate threat of a deadly virus.

Without getting too conspiratorial, there is no doubt in my mind that the sudden Covid outbreak in China killed the Hong Kong democracy movement. Was this a coincidence? Was the timing of the global pandemic dumb luck in China's favour? I honestly don't know. All I know is China came out on top.

But what I never imagined, while reporting on Chinese police busting protesters' heads in 2019, was that just months later, I would see police dressed in similar uniforms and using similar tactics create identical scenes in my own country.

I remember standing at the anti-lockdown protests in Melbourne the following year thinking, "Holy fuck. This really is déjà vu."

But before all of that, I died.

CHAPTER TWELVE

THE DAY I DIED

On the eve of Valentine's Day 2020, my heart stopped. I was clinically dead for a full five minutes.

I'm only here today because Rhonda - my wife, lover, and hero - performed lifesaving CPR that brought me back to life.

I had come home from the gym feeling a little unwell, but shrugged it off as nothing more than perhaps the after-effects of pushing myself too hard in training.

I made myself lunch consisting of a couple of steaks and some salad, at which Rhonda's friend who was visiting at the time joked: "That's a heart attack on a plate!"

The steaks had nothing to do with my cardiac arrest, so, to all the vegans reading this - sorry, but not sorry to disappoint you! But having said that, I can't help but laugh that our visitor made that comment right before my heart suddenly stopped.

After I'd eaten, I lay down for rest and told Rhonda I would wake up at 3pm to go to work. I woke up alright - in a hospital with tubes shoved down my throat. But I'm skipping ahead.

Rhonda had come into the bedroom at about 3.10pm to check on me and was shocked to find me still asleep. I'm a light sleeper, and I don't oversleep, especially not when I've got an interview scheduled and people waiting on me.

We know now that I would no longer be here if she had not checked on me. Another minute could have been too late. Something as simple as going to the bathroom before coming to wake me would have been fatal or, at the very least, caused me significant brain damage.

Rhonda found me in bed with my head on a funny angle, my face grey, and my eyes rolled back in my head.

Her instant reaction was to think that I was mucking around and playing a joke on her. This is the downside of being the class clown and consistently pranking my family. When you're actually dying of cardiac arrest, you need people to take you seriously.

It's a problem I've experienced throughout my life. Like that time I told you about earlier when I dislocated my shoulder as a kid, and none of my friends believed me.

Or the time I was playfighting in primary school and smashed my head into the concrete wall sending me into a fit of laughter as I held my hands to my head. All the kids thought it was hilarious, joining my contagious laughing. Until the blood started streaming through my hands, compressing the wound. Ten stitches later, no one thought it was funny.

Back to Rhonda.

She came closer to double-check and realised something was really wrong. When she saw the colour of my skin, she knew it was not a prank.

I'm good. I can fight through the pain of being pinched by dad while pretending to be unconscious without flinching.

But I'm not that good. I can't fake grey skin.

"Wake up Avi!" she yelled. And then, when I didn't respond, she repeated the command with even more urgency in her voice, increasing to a panic.

"Avi, wake up! Wake up!"

I wasn't responding at all.

Rhonda says she started to shake me, but nothing was happening. She became so terrified she started slapping me in the face, so hard, it turns out, that she felt guilty about it for days. And yet I still wasn't responding.

I cannot imagine what it would be like to find the person you love unconscious, unresponsive, and discoloured. I often wonder how I would have reacted had the tables been turned. A lot of people would probably have frozen, paralysed with fear.

Thank God my girl is a fighter.

Rhonda ran for a phone to call 000 (Australia's version of 911) and then raced back to the bedroom, where I was still lying unresponsive on the bed. But worse, by now, I wasn't breathing.

"You have to start CPR," the emergency operator urged, and she gave Rhonda directions over the phone.

Rhonda put the phone on speaker and started chest compressions – not bad for a girl whose medical expertise comprised a vague memory of a first aid course completed 13 years earlier when she had her first baby and a couple of TV episodes of House and ER.

They say about 90 per cent of people who experience an out-of-hospital cardiac arrest die, but CPR after cardiac arrest can double or triple a person's chance of survival if administered immediately.

Even with Rhonda's assistance, I was still much more likely to die than live.

The operator counted with Rhonda as she pumped my heart for eight minutes before help finally arrived.

It sends shivers down my spine, picturing the scenario. For those eight minutes, on the eve of that Valentine's Day, Rhonda was my heart. When her compressions slowed down, she would literally see what little bit of colour there was in my face drain away.

She will tell you that it was the longest eight minutes of her life.

It took the 17 first responders two hours to stabilise me before rushing me to the hospital in an induced coma.

I watched it all play out on our CCTV a month later. First, a fire truck arrived—they must have been closest. Then one ambulance after another, including MICA paramedics who provide advanced management of cardiac conditions.

It must have been a frightening scene for the entire street.

The whole saga was uncomfortably reminiscent of when I first fainted at school, except that this episode wasn't fake. It was surreal to watch the security footage later, seeing my lifeless body, surrounded by medics, rushed into an ambulance outside our home.

Even as they were racing me to the hospital, medics told Rhonda they expected the worst.

I might not live. And if I did live, they couldn't say for sure what effect the lack of oxygen would have on my brain.

Ambulance officers rushed me into the intensive care unit and began a series of tests. The tests provided good news. My arteries were good, and my heart seemed clear of damage.

Meanwhile, I was regaining consciousness and trying to understand where I was. As I opened my eyes, I started choking on the intubation tubes they'd shoved down my throat to allow me to breathe.

It felt so claustrophobic.

A nurse ran over and calmly explained the situation as she began pulling out the tubes.

"Hey there, we weren't expecting you back so quick. You're a lucky guy."

She told me what had happened and how Rhonda had saved my life.

"You had a cardiac arrest, and you died on your bedroom floor," she told me. "Your partner brought you back to life."

Doctors conducted numerous tests, concluding that I was in perfect health, notwithstanding that I had just suffered a cardiac arrest and died.

They explained how sudden cardiac arrest was one of the biggest killers of healthy and fit men under 40.

My cardiologist put it down to finally getting my kids back just days before suffering the medical episode.

"The stress you've experienced over the last year is the likely cause of your cardiac arrest," he advised.

It was also possible that a new pre-workout supplement I had taken to elevate my heart rate just hours earlier may have been the final nail in the coffin, so to speak.

A few days later, I was discharged from the hospital on strict conditions that I would not drive for six months and that I would take some time off work.

I was still working for TR News at this point. Tommy Robinson called me as soon as I got home.

"Bruv, take all the time you need. Don't worry about content. You'll be paid monthly for as long as you need," he reassured me. "Just get better".

Tommy's patience was a godsend because the recovery process was slow and arduous. My body was weak. I could hardly move. I was lethargic. I became skinny and unable to do much.

I spent weeks in bed before I was finally strong enough for Rhonda to take me on exciting excursions - to places like the supermarket, the bakery and the butcher. It felt great to finally be out of the house.

Little did I know in a few short months, the rest of the world would begin to get as enthusiastic by such expeditions as Covid restrictions forced everybody to stay home.

Speaking of my lifesaver, the only physical pain lingering after the heart attack was in my chest, where Rhonda had pumped my heart.

She joked that the pain remained there, so I would never forget that she had saved my life.

We planned not to tell the children about my near-death experience because we didn't want to scare them. But when Rhonda's nine-year-old son asked if I'd "died a little bit", I couldn't lie.

The kid read me like a book, so I told him what had happened.

And then he asked me the obvious question …

"Did you see the light?"

I answered him honestly.

"I didn't see anything."

Straight-faced, without hesitance and in his typical charming smart-ass tone replied: "Oh well, that makes sense. There's no way *you're* going to heaven."

That was the first good laugh I'd enjoyed in a while. It hurt my already aching chest but was well worth it.

Barely recovering from her son's hilarious response to my death, I went to say good night to Rhonda's 13-year-old daughter.

"Goodnight!" I said as she carefully hugged me so as not to inflict any further unnecessary pain.

"Guess what, Avi," she said softly with a twinkle in her eye.

"What?" I asked.

"Well, now you can never leave my mother. You literally owe her your life."

She had a great point. But I was looking at it differently. I thought, "Score! There's no way Rhonda will leave *me* now. She's too invested!"

And with those jokes, surrounded by love, my road to recovery began.

There's nothing like losing your life to make you appreciate it, and nothing like almost losing your family to make you treasure them that much more.

CHAPTER THIRTEEN

VICTORIA POLICE APOLOGISE

Attending protests was now my bread and butter. With the advent of 'woke' social justice warriors, there seemed to be a new protest every other weekend in Melbourne. If people weren't protesting against climate change, they were protesting to expand LBGTQ rights, or some other lefty progressivist cause.

My 'schtick' has usually been to turn up somewhere and simply ask questions. Whether I agree with someone or not, I've always enjoyed interacting with people. Essentially it is just me having fun with a camera crew in tow. Live interviews at protests are something I've always loved doing. And people love watching them.

What amazed me, though, was how little most protesters typically knew about the issues they were protesting. Their arguments were almost always emotional, so I quickly realised I could outsmart them by knowing even a few simple facts about the issues involved.

As you already know, I'm not the most educated guy in the country, and I certainly don't think I'm the smartest. But I had a simple formula that worked.

Each week I'd look at the far-left wing protests scheduled, and as I was heading into the city, I would spend about five minutes researching the issue. I would then rock up to their demonstrations and poke holes in their arguments by applying common sense.

These interactions, filmed and posted online, were typically hilarious and highly embarrassing for the activists. But I'd often regret not spending more time researching the topic because, as entertaining as the content was, I realised later how much better it could have been.

What I didn't know about issues before I conducted the protest interviews, I quickly learnt after the rally via the comments on my videos.

For example, as I headed to the George Floyd Black Lives Matter (BLM) protest in 2020, I spent a few minutes researching the background and quickly realised the angle. These people were out protesting in support of a career criminal with a very violent history who was high on drugs when he died in dodgy circumstances at the hands of police. On top of that, he was American. And I knew that none of them would even know the name of an Australian shot dead by the same Minnesota police force two years earlier.

Unlike George Floyd, Justine Damond was completely innocent. She'd called the police to report the possible assault of a woman in an alley behind her house, and the attending officer gunned her down.

The difference, of course, was that Damond was a white victim who died at the hands of a black cop, rather than the other way around. Sadly she never saw justice. Unlike the officers involved in George Floyd's fatal arrest, her killer was released.

So I decided to go around the BLM protest, asking protestors if they knew about Justine Damond. None of them did. And I showed the world how ridiculous these Aussies were protesting for an American criminal whose killers were certainly being held accountable. Yet, they did not even know the name of their fellow Australian who was gunned down in a far more straightforward case with no natural justice forthcoming.

As good as my video was at the time, it could have been better. The talking point many protesters referred to was black deaths in custody in Australia.

A lot of them marched holding signs condemning the '432 black deaths in custody'. Only after releasing the video did I educate myself on that little lie.

Firstly, Aboriginals are less likely to die in police custody and the prison system than non-Aboriginals. Since 1991, indigenous people have made up 19% of all deaths in Australian prisons. In proportion to their actual numbers in jail (27%), that's considerably less.

A breakdown of the causes of death sheds more light on the subject. In prison, roughly 10 indigenous people die per year. Most of them die from natural causes (58%)—another 37% from suicides and drug overdoses. Deaths from external trauma (usually prison fights) account for the remaining 5%.

The number of Aboriginal deaths in 'police custody' amount to approximately 6 per year. Of this number, 56% have been in incidents where police were not in direct contact - a further 21% die from natural causes and 19% die from self-inflicted injuries.

If I had known these facts before the Melbourne BLM protests, I could have destroyed their narrative, on camera, in seconds. That was a repeating regret I had.

While getting millions of views was great, failing to fully show the obvious flaws in their argument felt like a missed opportunity.

As I became well known, and as 'woke' protesters became wary of being embarrassed, local Antifa members (a self-proclaimed Anti-fascist group) planned strategies to try to intimidate me.

My job was to ask them to explain why they were protesting. Their job, apparently, was to surround me, yelling "wife-beater" in an attempt to ruin my footage.

Their tactics never worked because, their behaviour gave me a story, every single time, even if there was nothing else to report on.

The kerfuffle they created not only made them look silly, it gave me backup content in case the rest of my interviews weren't great. Thanks to them, I got two great videos at most protests. One video would be me interviewing protestors, and the other video would be of the mob trying to intimidate me. People loved watching both.

Before I pleaded guilty to a crime I didn't commit, the mob would yell "Nazi" at me. This was always amusing, since I was usually wearing a religious Kippah. I did not need to defend myself against the charge, and the video would speak for itself.

But then the clowns hit the jackpot when I was convicted for a crime I never committed for the sake of my children.

Engaging on that issue, at the time, was more complicated. I couldn't defend myself for legal reasons, nor could I act like domestic violence was okay.

But luckily for me, my detractors always acted so crazily. Even though people watching online didn't know the truth or the context behind their slurs, no one took them seriously.

I would calmly tell those punters who were attacking me: "You don't know anything about my personal life. But let's pretend you do. Now that you've called me a wife-beater, let's get onto the things you're protesting about."

It would work when even they got bored of screaming about my ex-wife. And they typically knew even less about the issues they were protesting than they knew about my personal life.

Well, that would often just make them get more aggressive because, obviously, they didn't want to talk about actual issues. They couldn't talk about real issues. It was easier to slander me. As protesters became more agitated toward me, police would move in and, in a classic case of blaming the victim, demand I be the one to move on.

This always struck me as incredibly unfair. Antifa thugs would threaten violence, and I would be forcibly removed in order to 'keep the peace'. Antifa couldn't use personal sledges to shut me up, so they used the Victorian police, allegedly for my safety, who kept sidelining me.

The officers would claim they had a right to move me on to prevent a peace breach and ensure my safety. But I wasn't worried about my safety. I was concerned about reporting what was going on at protests.

It kept happening, so I got legal advice. It turned out that the police didn't actually have the power to move me on. I printed out the relevant law to show police officers proving there were exemptions to the move-on orders, allowing me to continue doing my job as a reporter. But police simply ignored me. Again and again, I was viewed as the problem, and was moved on.

The first time Victoria Police arrested me at a protest was on Australia Day 2020. Covid hadn't yet changed the country's course, so social justice activists were out in full force protesting against Australia's national holiday. The anti-Australia Day protests have become an Australia Day tradition.

I was interviewing demonstrators demanding that Australia Day be moved to a different date, but, funnily enough, they couldn't tell me what happened on January 26 to make that date so terrible.

When pushed, they all seemed to think it was the day "Captain Cook invaded Australia".

Again, here were these passionate individuals, protesting an issue but having no idea of the basic facts.

Australia Day marks the arrival of the First Fleet in January 1788, which Captain Arthur Phillip commanded. Captain Cook had been dead for nine years at that point.

It became pretty evident to me that the date wasn't even the issue, as they'd likely protest any new date as well.

"Do you want to change the date or abolish Australia Day," I'd ask.

"Both," several protesters would answer.

"You can't have both. If you change the date, by definition, you're not abolishing it," I'd point out.

And without fail, they'd all opt for abolishing the date.

Giving these protesters a platform would show they wanted Australia Day cancelled because they simply hated Australia.

Police saw me interviewing people and immediately arrested me, handcuffing and detaining me for half an hour to "prevent a breach of the peace". They ignored my protestations that the legislation they relied on to arrest me contained exemptions that should have allowed me to continue my reporting.

In the following months, Victoria Police would use the same tactics – not to stop Antifa thugs from committing violence, but to shut me up and stop me from embarrassing the Victorian State Government.

Under the direction of Victorian Premier Daniel Andrews, Melbourne's harsh Covid lockdowns made world headlines. The premier banned Victorians from travelling more than 5km from their own homes. Schools and playgrounds were closed, businesses shut down, and people's lives were devastated.

Victoria Police enforced the government restrictions with a zealotry eerily akin to what I had seen from Chinese Police in Hong Kong. They were brutal. Police arrested people who had never been in trouble with the law for posting messages on Facebook, walking in the park, and failing to wear masks.

The lockdowns sparked massive protests, and police reacted with a level of force we had never before seen in our country. Gone were the traditional blue police uniforms, they had been replaced by black paramilitary outfits designed for intimidation and control.

Police used tear gas and, ultimately, shot at citizens with rubber bullets for nothing more than daring to protest government health policies. It was about as un-Australian as you can imagine.

I was covering one of the lockdown protests at Melbourne's Albert Park on September 5, 2020, when police arrested me for a second time.

I was surrounded and manhandled, thrown to the ground by multiple officers dressed in combat gear, and placed tightly in handcuffs.

It was intense. I'd never experienced anything close to this takedown by authoritarian thugs, not even while reporting in Hong Kong. Even there, they left me alone and stuck to brutalising their dissident population.

I couldn't believe what had just happened.

However, this time police had gone too far and messed with the wrong journalist because I had just begun working for Rebel News.

My previous, much less violent arrest happened while I was working for Tommy Robinson. And when police got away with that crime, they made it their official tactic. Move Avi on, or arrest him. That was their clear strategy for dealing with me.

But by September 5, 2020, I joined Rebel News (A Canadian run media organisation). And lucky for me, Rebel had the means, know-how and willingness to handle these situations. My new boss, Ezra Levant, immediately said we should sue for damages. And, while we were at it, we would include the unfair Australia Day arrest in our claim against Victoria Police.

We filed a suit accusing them of false imprisonment, battery and hindering my legal journalism work. It was essential to do this because allowing the arrests to stand would have allowed mainstream media to use them to delegitimise everything I did.

Mainstream media used the fact that police arrested me for a second time as proof I was not a real journalist and as an argument that Rebel News was not a legitimate news outlet. Of course, they would claim that. Not because it was true but because we were taking too many eyeballs off their fake news.

How dare a bloke with no formal media training do a better job than the legacy media during a lockdown. And unlike the mainstream media, I wasn't simply repeating the government line and demonising citizens.

When the Canberra Times reported my action against police, they called me a "right-wing activist" who "claimed" to be a journalist. They called Rebel News a "conservative" outlet that had "peddled conspiracy theories against climate change and Islam".

The mainstream media weren't interested in the truth any more than the police seemed interested in the law.

But my court action didn't deter the police at first.

They knew who I was and were clearly targeting me. I was arrested for a third time on January 26, 2021, while interviewing Australia Day protesters—a protest sanctioned by police despite the rest of the population being banned from gathering in public because of Covid restrictions.

Apparently, the virus knew to differentiate between social justice and anti-lockdown protests. It was super clever like that.

Half a dozen police forcibly led me away from the protest to once again avoid a "breach of the peace". This was despite the fact that my only 'crime' had been to interview people who wanted to be interviewed.

Officers then detained me against a fence until a police van arrived to take me away. It was incredible.

I showed them my accredited press card, issued by the federal government's Department of Home Affairs. But they weren't interested.

I asked them how I was breaching the peace. But they wouldn't answer.

Police kept insisting I wasn't under arrest, just being detained.

"If I'm not under arrest, I'm going to leave," I responded.

"No, you can't," they ordered.

I asked them how they could detain me if I was not being arrested, and again, they would not answer me.

When a police van arrived, they forced me into the back of a divvy van and locked the door.

Remember, I was not under arrest. So, I could only conclude that Victoria Police were kidnapping me.

Weirdly, they drove me around for about half an hour before dropping me randomly in the suburb of Caufield.

"Am I being charged with anything?" I asked the cops as they let me out of the van.

"We are just the transport, mate," an officer replied, before they drove off, leaving me stranded on the side of the road.

I still have no idea why they dropped me off in Caufield. I don't live anywhere near there. And they know my address as they previously visited my home in an attempt to intimidate me into not covering lockdown protests. The only reason that makes any sense to me is that it's a known Jewish area. Was that some sort of message? Were Jews to just stay in their own ghetto?

I knew that police on the ground had clearly been given instructions to target me.

Video of the incident went viral, not just in Australia but around the world, exposing Victoria for the socialist police state it had become.

After over two years in court, police were eventually forced into issuing me with a public apology, not just for that incident, but for all three arrests.

In July of 2022, Victoria Police Superintendent Craig Thornton issued the following statement:

"On January 26, 2020, at about 1.10pm Mr Yemini was arrested by members of Victoria Police while conducting numerous video interviews with 'Pay The Rent' protesters and other members of the public gathered in Melbourne's CBD. Mr Yemini was detained and escorted from the area.

"On September 5, 2020, at about 2.40pm Mr Yemini Was arrested by members of Victoria Police whilst conducting numerous video interviews and recording events at the 'Lockout Law' rally at Albert Park. Mr Yemini was detained for a short period of time after his arrest.

"On January 26, 2021, Mr Yemini was detained by members of Victoria Police whilst conducting video interviews and recording events with protesters and other members of the public gathered in the Melbourne CBD. Mr Yemini was detained and driven to Caulfield.

"On each occasion, Mr. Yemini was wrongly arrested and detained by members of Victoria Police while reporting for Rebel News.

"Victoria Police sincerely apologises for the hurt and embarrassment suffered by Mr Yemini on January 26 2020, September 5 2020 and January 26 2021 as a consequence of the arrests and subsequent detention.»

I could easily have taken money from the state as compensation. My security guard, arrested while working for me at an anti-lockdown protest in 2021, was paid a six-figure settlement for his single unlawful arrest.

Imagine what they would have given me for all three incidents.

The government would have paid any amount of money rather than issue that apology. But I didn't want money. What's the point of having a million dollars in your pocket if you are bound by a non-disclosure agreement that prevents you from saying anything negative about police? What sort of a journalist would I have been to accept that?

My security guard deserved every cent he got. But my job is to expose the truth, and I wasn't about to let a payout hinder that – no matter how large the amount.

The apology was humiliating for Victoria Police. Not once, not twice, but they had wrongfully arrested the same journalist three times.

Once we'd consented to the general terms of the settlement, it took three months to agree on the wording of the apology and another five months for them to get "reporting for Rebel News" approved by the top brass at Victoria Police.

While it was hard for them to admit fault three times, it was even more challenging for them to admit I was a legitimate reporter.

The backdown represented not only vindication for me personally but afforded me a license now to do my job without the threat of police harassment. From day one, I only wanted the ability to do my job. And with that apology from police, I could get back to reporting the injustices done to others, instead of worrying about the injustices done to me.

Oh, and I could finally get back to reporting left-wing protests.

Since the apology, I have received red-carpet treatment from police, even in hostile crowds. And from this point, I plan on putting in the effort to research the issues more thoroughly.

CHAPTER FOURTEEN

FIGHT THE FINES

I wasn't the only person victimised by Victoria Police during the pandemic. The fact is that thousands of people were fined for ridiculous things, and to make matters worse, the mainstream media largely stayed silent about it. When they did speak up, it was often to mock the person being fined.

So much for their claims of "speaking truth to power".

I knew first-hand what it was like to be falsely accused and how difficult it was to fight back. Even with the resources of Rebel News behind me, taking on the government was expensive, time-consuming and intimidating.

How must ordinary people, without the backing of an international news organisation, have felt?

A few months before my joining Rebel News, they'd launched a campaign to fight for the average joe in Canada unfairly fined for breaking arbitrary Covid restrictions. They started with a pastor who had dared to feed the homeless during lockdown.

So as soon as I joined the team, we launched the 'Fight the Fines' campaign Down Under. The idea was to crowd-fund lawyers for Australians who wanted to fight back against their outrageous Covid related fines.

At the time, I had no idea that 'Fight the Fines' would become the work I would grow most proud of.

When Covid first hit, like most rational people, I was happy to stay home and even wear a mask. Heck, the virus seemed incredibly frightening. After two elderly great uncles, one in Israel and another in New York, had died with Covid, I began encouraging my followers to take personal responsibility.

Even though I believed Covid was a deadly virus, from the beginning, I wasn't keen on government intervention to enforce measures to protect our health.

But then, as we learnt more and the government became entangled in a web of lies as they declared a state of emergency to enact more extraordinary powers, I realised something was seriously wrong.

I couldn't believe the broad powers they were giving themselves.

I asked a lawyer friend to help me comprehend if I understood things correctly.

"Under a state of emergency, can the police really enter your home without a warrant?" I asked.

"Yes," he answered. "If they suspect you may be a risk to public health."

"How far can they go?" I questioned.

"It's pretty broad. But that's why there's a maximum of six months in total that the State of Emergency can be extended," he added, trying to reassure me.

My friend explained that our legal system had prepared for this exact scenario. And that's why they capped it.

"Legislation like this is drawn up in peacetime so that in the stress of war, so to speak, governments don't make irrational decisions," my mate said.

I was right to be sceptical as that "maximum six months" was repealed with new legislation "in the stress of war" by a power-hungry dictator who managed to lock us down for almost two years.

In mid-2020, things got incredibly crazy. The legacy media acted as cheerleaders for authoritarian rule—the same media which had condemned China months earlier for similar breaches of human rights in Hong Kong.

But it wasn't only the mainstream media that went missing as public freedoms were trashed. Human rights and civil liberty organisations were nowhere to be seen either.

Rebel News in Canada, and now Australia, were determined to help turn the tide against the abusive fines and lockdowns that negatively affected so many people.

I understood there were reasonable limits that the public needed to accept to fight the pandemic, but governments had gone too far.

Premier Daniel Andrews in his infamous daily press conferences, added absurd new rules even instituting a 9pm curfew for some time, restricting our lives further. Whether overzealous inspectors, police who just didn't understand the new rules, bureaucrats trying to scare the public, or politicians enjoying their "emergency" powers a little too much, there were just too many unreasonable fines issued.

Someone had to defend people's civil liberties. And unfortunately, there was no one else left to do it.

I began advertising for people who had received an outrageous fine to contact us.

I also advertised for people willing to donate money to help pay people's legal bills.

Individually, the battle for civil liberties was too big. But together, we could fight the fines and restore people's reputations. And we did.

Outrageous stories from across the country quickly inundated us. I got straight to work.

I'm not going to lie. It felt great.

I got to tell incredible stories of public interest that the mainstream media were ignoring. In addition, I got to actively help people who had been let down by the civil liberties organisations that were supposed to help them.

I felt like this was what being a Rebel News reporter was supposed to be.

Weirdly enough, just like in Canada, our first case also happened to be a pastor. He'd received a bunch of fines for encouraging people to 'exercise their rights'. Basically, protesting the restrictions without breaking them—but even his religious profession didn't save him.

My second case broke my heart. A man who was already down on his luck, in-between jobs and experiencing homelessness for the first time, received a fine for allegedly breaching lockdown curfew for sleeping in his car.

Two police approached Daniel's parked car wanting to know why he was breaching the strict 9pm Covid curfew by being in his vehicle rather than in his house.

Daniel politely explained to the police that his car was his house.

Police refused to listen, and fined the homeless man $1,652. He was issued a ticket for his misfortune. Essentially, he was fined for being homeless!

Daniel contested the fine on his own, supplying police with a letter from his doctor certifying that he was "being treated for a long-term mental illness" and that "he is currently homeless".

Police wrote back: "Your circumstances have been considered, and in this instance, this offence is considered to be a serious safety-related matter."

The fine would stand.

I was outraged when I heard his story. I knew first-hand what it was like to be homeless, a situation I wouldn't wish on my worst enemy.

And I couldn't imagine being fined for sleeping in a car when you had nowhere else to be.

We broadcast an interview with the man and set him up with the same lawyer who successfully represented me in my cases against Victoria Police.

Daniel's fine was eventually withdrawn.

We continued to fight these fines and continued to win.

Case after case, the distressed victim would contact us after police rejected their internal review telling them their fines would not be withdrawn. And, with the help of viewers we took up people's causes.

Kerry Cotterill's case was infuriating. The grandmother used her lawful hour of exercise to walk alone in the permitted 5km radius carrying a sign in protest of Daniel Andrews. An idea I imagine she got from the pastor in Sydney before police charged him.

Kerry was fined $1,652 for breaching the rules, even though the state couldn't point to any specific restriction she was breaking.

As in Daniel's case, police rejected her initial request to have the matter withdrawn through an internal review.

Her matter was so outrageous that our legal team thought it would be a great test case in a constitutional challenge. We wanted the chance for the Supreme Court to rule on the implied right of political communication.

You'd think in a free and democratic country, the right to protest would be a given. Especially when protesting alone without breaching any of the overreaching restrictions imposed by out-of-control governments.

As soon as we filed, the state withdrew Kerry's fine and submitted to the Supreme Court that Kerry no longer had standing as the penalty had been removed.

That's how scared they were.

They had no idea if they'd win or lose. Sadly, after a two-year battle, we lost that challenge.

As I write this book, not a single constitutional challenge to the Covid tyranny has succeeded in Australia.

I guess it should have been obvious. Courts generally don't like ruling against the state. And the fact that the restrictions did not affect judges, as they did the rest of us, made it even easier for them to rule against us.

Just like politicians, judges got to work through the pandemic. And like the politicians in parliament, they had it better, not even having to travel to court.

To this point, all our wins have come from challenging the fines at the Magistrates Court level.

Like in Daniel's case, the state withdrew most fines at different stages in the Magistrates Court process; some even on the day of the trial.

And just like Daniel and Kerry, almost every person who joined our 'Fight the Fines' initiative was grateful. They'd tell me how they couldn't have done it without legal representation, and they were right. I received a lot of emails from people who self-represented and failed, looking to see if we could help with their appeals.

But it's not over yet. Between Canada and Australia, Rebel News took on more than 2,500 cases. And Down Under, we still have a handful that the government don't want to let go.

A mother who had her four-year-old child ripped from her arms as police forced her into the back of a police van almost three years ago for 'exercising her rights' is still fighting her fines in the Magistrates Court after losing her constitutional battle in the NSW Supreme Court.

In her case, the state of New South Wales has not withdrawn her fine. So after losing the Supreme Court Challenge, we now have to fight on the facts in the Magistrates Court.

And she's not alone.

The owners of a small coffee shop also in NSW are still awaiting trial two years after being fined for serving customers without a mask. They had exemptions on the day. And even though it's not at the top of people's minds, I take pride in being by their side until the end.

As I said, this initiative is something I will be proud of for the rest of my life.

CHAPTER FIFTEEN

TROUBLE ACROSS THE DITCH

If the treatment I received from Victoria Police wasn't bad enough, it was as if the New Zealand government heard about it and said: "Hold my beer."

While planning a trip to New Zealand to report on an anti-government protest in August 2022, I also scheduled interviews with some of the most lied-about personalities in that country.

I thought one of them, independent commentator Chantelle Baker – a woman often crucified by New Zealand's press - deserved to tell her story. I called Chantelle and locked in a time to interview her while I was there.

Chantelle took to Telegram, informing her followers that we were crossing the ditch to give the anti-mandate protesters a fair hearing. I didn't ask her not to share the news, even though I probably should have forecasted the reaction.

Like clockwork, the mainstream media went to town on news of my impending arrival.

"Parliament protest: Australian conspiracy commentators to attend event, claims NZ influencer," the New Zealand Herald headline read.

Of course they were worried. The last thing the mainstream media wanted to see in New Zealand was a repeat of what happened in Australia - Rebel News opening people's eyes to mainstream media lies.

Throughout Covid, the media controlled the narrative, and were well paid by the Jacinda Ardern government for doing so.

I'm not kidding. The Ardern government spent at least NZ$105 million in media bribes throughout Covid. Controversially, first on a support package of $50M for "ailing" mainstream media groups to survive Covid.

"This support reflects the essential role media play at this time in delivering access to reliable and up-to-date news coverage and keeping New Zealanders connected while in lockdown," communications minister Kris Faafoi said when the money was announced.

"There is evidence New Zealanders are turning to trusted news sources in record numbers at this time so it is critical the media is supported to keep doing the great job they have been doing."

Faafoi said he chose proposals that "get support out the door as fast as possible".

And if that wasn't weird enough - most media companies thrived during the pandemic since the average person was glued to the news. The Ardern government created a $55m "public interest journalism fund" but you had to agree with the government's position on several contentious issues to qualify for a share of the dosh.

The media in New Zealand was bought and paid for during Covid. There was no free press, and that's why they were willing to do anything to stop us from coming.

After reading the New Zealand Herald's hit piece, I retained a lawyer and immigration agent just to ensure we were doing everything by the book, and was advised we were good to go.

I arrived at Melbourne airport with a colleague on August 22, 2022. As I reached the Qantas check-in counter, the lady scanned my passport.

"Oh," she reacted. "I've never seen this!"

I assumed it had something to do with my new passport, which I was using for the first time.

"I need to get my manager to help on this one," she said.

She walked to the last counter and began chatting with another lady whom I presumed was in charge. I stood waiting at the check-in counter as Qantas staff made phone calls before eventually coming back to me with the phone in hand.

"New Zealand immigration wants to ask some questions," she said.

"Sure," I answered as I took the mobile from her.

The New Zealand immigration official on the other end of the line began with the sort of general questions you might expect.

But then suddenly, the agent said, "I've just looked at an article online that says you were convicted for a violent crime and therefore I am exercising my power to refuse you entry into New Zealand today".

I protested on the phone, ensuring she understood that my conviction was for a minor assault for which I was fined $1600 and certainly not jailed for twelve months as per the threshold justifying a ban.

But she wasn't having a bar of it and refused my entry.

The next day, Kiwi Prime Minister Jacinta Ardern claimed to have nothing to do with the decision to ban me from the country. She told a press conference: "I understand that it is solely for immigration, and it is not something I had any awareness of until I saw some commentary online."

Yeah right.

New Zealand immigration was quick to publicly blame a criminal conviction that clearly didn't reach the legal threshold to refuse a person entry to the country. But that didn't stop the mainstream media from running with that lie.

Later, a leaked Interpol communication revealed that New Zealand police had requested immigration officials ban me from coming to report on anti-government protests.

Heavily redacted documents, obtained under Freedom of Information laws, showed that immigration officials had been instructed, ahead of my arrival in the country, to assess my reasons for travel "with a view to having them (us) turned away at the border".

The documents went on to say: "That (having me deported) is the intention but an assessment is required by border staff at the time."

Incredibly, the document said that "no information has been received yet to confirm that the subjects have in fact made bookings to travel to NZ".

In a nutshell, they didn't even know if we were coming to New Zealand. But their intention was to ban us if we ever did. Of course, they were careful to remind border control that they needed to go through the motions and pretend to assess our reasons for travel before refusing us entry as had been pre-determined.

The reason for our ban had nothing to do with my minor criminal conviction. The internal immigration document instead referred to "the propensity for both individuals to incite and agitate people with opposing views".

The implications were mind-blowing. New Zealand, a so-called democracy, secretly planned to ban journalists the government didn't like from entering the country because they held "opposing views".

That should have worried everyone, even my detractors. Those who celebrated the New Zealand government's decision because they hated my politics ought to have considered that a conservative government might one day apply the same precedent to their left-wing views. Sadly, I have found that many on the left care much more about sides than about principles.

Once they managed to ban a journalist they claimed would incite and agitate people with opposing views, the New Zealand government officials celebrated.

A leaked email from immigration authorities to border control staff said: "Great work from the border control team. I have been advised that Yemini was refused entry into New Zealand and turned around at the border. Excellent work!"

Immigration officials told the media that the onus was on me to prove that my conviction did not reach the threshold to refuse an Australian entry to the country. That was disingenuous since they knew full well that my sentence did not meet the threshold, and I didn't need to tell them.

According to their own guidelines, the threshold was having been convicted of an offence and sentenced to 12 months or more in prison anytime in the past 10 years. They knew that my conviction was a summary offence, so minor it had incurred only a $1600 fine.

They knew this because a leaked email from Interpol New Zealand showed that they had already been in contact with Australian authorities prior to my travel, fishing for information that could be used against me.

In the email, they wrote:

"NZ police would like to stop the two (my colleague and I) from entering the country and urgently seek any information regarding criminal convictions or any information tending to show they are individuals of bad character, associated to criminal groups and individuals or far-right extremism groups."

Almost word-for-word, copied and pasted from the initial article published by The New Zealand Herald without a byline.

Australian authorities advised: "Took some leverage but I can confirm the assault was a true conviction. With conviction fined $1600. Trust this assists you."

So New Zealand immigration officials knew that my conviction was not enough to keep me out of the country and yet used it as their justification anyway. That was an indictment not only on the New Zealand government but also on the mainstream media.

Jacinta Ardern's government was so confident that the mainstream media would repeat their lie without ever bothering to check if it was true or not, that they didn't hesitate to use it against me.

The Kiwi government's faith was duly rewarded.

Newshub reported: "Far right conspiracy theorist Avi Yemini denied entry into New Zealand because of criminal conviction."

Crikey's website ran with the headline: "Right-wing commentator Avi Yemini denied entry to New Zealand over domestic abuse conviction."

And New Zealand's One News told readers: "Conviction sees Aus YouTuber barred from NZ ahead of protest."

None of it was true. And those media outlets have never corrected the record. Worse, they have never bothered to hold the conspirators to account.

But they messed with the wrong person. They should have asked my mum. I don't fold easily. I'm persistent.

They're still dragging their feet in the hope I will give up but I won't. Because I will jump through every hoop, and I will win.

If they had let me in that day, I would have covered the protest and conducted a few interviews. It would have been over before they knew it.

Now, thanks to their corrupt collusion to ban me, I've gained a much larger following in New Zealand.

And when my visa is finally approved, a much larger audience will be watching my New Zealand report.

In December 2022, when applying for a visa, I was ordered to get a fingerprint and namecheck from the Australian Federal Police, even though they already had those records.

When I asked why this was necessary, they told me it was for formal documentation.

My lawyer advised that this was not true. They just knew that it would take two months for the appointment. It was another stalling tactic. But I did it, and we've finally submitted it.

Now we wait for them to overturn the unlawful ban.

If they refuse my visa, we'll be heading to court. I can't file proceedings until that point. But after seeing the internal communications, I'm willing to bet everything that they won't risk it. They don't want these corrupt officials cross-examined under oath.

I can confidently say Kia ora New Zealand in 2023.

See you soon.

CHAPTER SIXTEEN

FIGHTING FOR TRUTH

If it wasn't for social media, I wouldn't exist because, let's face it, there is little chance that someone with my background would have successfully gotten through the traditional media channels. But it's not just people obstructed by the mainstream media, it is the truth that is continually bullied and blocked.

I first learnt about the legacy media's causal relationship with the truth when I began promoting my gyms around Melbourne. In order to generate publicity, I would send media releases commenting on all sorts of issues and promoting myself as the go-to guy for commentary on self-defence and even counter-terrorism issues.

It was ridiculous, and I knew it was absurd because I wasn't an expert on any of that. I just happened to own a self-defence gym where I wasn't even an instructor. My ownership of the gym, along with three years in the Israeli army, meant the media could justify treating me like I was some kind of authority.

My point is that the legacy media are lazy - really lazy. They mostly rely on press releases fed from government departments or corporations and repeat them without much research or thought.

IDF Training became one of the most well-known gyms nationwide because I pumped out weekly press releases that the media would simply regurgitate.

Institutions pay millions to PR companies to do what I figured out for free. Create a story based on current events, throw in some outrageous "expert" comments, and hey, presto! The mainstream media will often print your press release almost word for word.

The other thing I learnt about journalists is that they don't want to bite the hand that feeds them. So, in Dan Andrews' Victoria, reporters are reluctant to be too hard on the government if it means they risk no longer being spoon-fed stories.

Stepping out of line has real-life consequences. For example, Daniel Andrews, via the house speaker, decides which journalists get media passes for the parliament in Victoria. If you don't toe the line, you're out.

And I certainly don't toe the line, so, was physically dragged out of the Premier's press conference in parliament. We then spent almost $300k challenging my ban in The Supreme Court of Victoria.

I lost.

Daniel Andrews didn't argue that I was not a legitimate journalist. Instead, he relied on parliamentary privilege, arguing that the court had no jurisdiction to decide who could or could not attend parliamentary press conferences.

It's a unique part of the law designed to protect the integrity of our democracy by ensuring the courts cannot interfere with the process of legislating.

For example, suppose the speaker kicked a member out of the chambers for causing some disruption. In that case, that member cannot go to the courts to overrule the speaker's decision.

But we argued that the Premier's powers did not extend to press conferences simply because they're held on parliament grounds.

For example, suppose an MP held a party in his office at parliament and refused to pay the caterer. In that case, the caterer could go to the courts for a resolution.

As I told you before, I've learnt the hard way that our courts rarely over-rule the state.

Now I have to pay damages, and the court has ratified that the supreme leader gets the final say on who reports from our state's corridors of power.

That's not how a free press should work. But then again, Victoria is far from free.

Daniel Andrews often takes a media entourage overseas, but you must be invited. If you've gotten the government offside, the Premier's Department will not invite you. So, to stay in the Premier's good books and remain eligible for essential trips, you must avoid asking difficult questions.

It's better for a journalist's career to just report whatever the government says without ever asking uncomfortable questions. That's the way it works in Dan Andrews' Victoria.

You have to remember that journalists are just ordinary people. They want to experience the perks of the job and the opportunities as much as the next person.

Let me give you another example of media complicity.

Think about the climate summits held every year around the world. Instead of challenging the things said at these World Economic Forum (WEF), COP27 meetings or whatever, the media just repeat them.

When I attended the WEF for the first time in 2022, it became clear how incestuous the relationship between globalists and the media was - a bit like the New Zealand government and their press.

Everywhere I turned, there was a mainstream media or big-tech advertisement. Journalists from some of the most prominent publications were on the schedule to give talks about how they could help the WEF to spread its message.

I bumped into the New York Times Deputy Managing Editor, Rebecca Blumenstein, having coffee in Davos, and asked her:

"How is the public meant to believe the New York Times is here to actually ask the tough questions when you're here as an invited guest?"

She refused to answer because there was no good answer she could give.

The good news is that social media has revolutionised the political and media scene because it has allowed everyone to ask questions and reach millions of people.

That's why somebody like me - and organisations like Rebel News - are so important. It's the emerging media, rather than the legacy media, who are willing to ask the hard questions and disrupt the status quo.

Some politicians and journalists view the emerging media as a threat, because we are. And, as I have learnt, they will demean and defame us, trying their hardest to distort perceptions to discredit and sideline us.

Whether it's my arrests at protests, or my banning from New Zealand, or my minor conviction for a crime I didn't commit, they will tell part of the story but deliberately leave other pieces out to kill you off as their competition.

They'll call you "far right" or "controversial".

They'll refer to you as an "activist" rather than as a journalist.

They'll bring up your past, even though it has absolutely nothing to do with the issue at hand.

They'll do anything to keep you quiet.

Platforms like Rebel News give people options they previously didn't have. Instead of switching on to mainstream television to get their news, people watch us because they know we don't self-censor (at least not on our website).

But telling the truth increasingly requires you to use your wits because it can quickly get you banned from platforms you need to reach people.

Remember that in Davos, all the big-tech companies were there too.

I was banned from Facebook a few years ago for supposed hate speech. Of course, the great irony is that many of my detractors use that exact same platform to spread hate about me. I'm banned, but they are still there. Go figure.

About two years ago, I decided to start from scratch and give Facebook another go. Having learnt my lesson about what you can and cannot say on that particular platform, I thought I would launch a brand-new page and just say things according to Facebook's guidelines while allowing my audience to read between the lines.

By the way, I'm a great believer in the intelligence of my audience. People are bright, and sometimes you don't have to tell them absolutely everything. Sometimes you can give them enough to join the dots for themselves without getting yourself into trouble. Anyway, I created a new Facebook page and attracted a whopping 170,000 followers in only 12 weeks. I was amazed. Facebook was going to take off for me again.

On a Friday afternoon, the platform verified my page. By the Monday, they monetised me. And then, on the Tuesday, I was banned.

By Wednesday, a far-left 'journalist', who has an unhealthy obsession with me, had taken credit for my ban.

"After Gizmodo contacted Facebook about whether Yemini — whose Facebook page had been previously banned by Facebook — was breaking the rules with his new page, the company confirmed that they had banned Yemini's new page," Cam Wilson, who now fixates over me at Crikey, wrote for Gizmodo at the time.

Facebook notified me that I was in breach of their recidivism policy, which means that if you open a new page with the same name as a previously banned page, it will be banned all over again—even if you don't breach any of their terms of service.

That means if I ever open a page in my name, Avi Yemini, it'll get banned. With no end date. For life.

You get less time for murder than you do for breaching Facebook's guidelines. Hate speech is a very subjective thing, but you can never repent, and there is no redemption. Once you breach the rules, you're done.

Facebook is not the only corporation now an expert at cancel culture. It seems like businesses everywhere are scared to death by any kind of criticism, legitimate or not.

And they don't just go after the person who allegedly said the wrong thing. Activists - by which I mean hateful people with Twitter accounts - go after anyone associated with the person who committed the original thought crime.

They destroy the character of the person they don't like, and then they say, 'oh, look who he's friends with', and go after them too.

British women's rights activist Kellie-Jay Keen, also known as Posie Parker, knows how that feels. The entire Australian establishment joined together to assassinate her character after Nazis gate crashed her Let Women Speak event in Melbourne. When I asked her about allegations that she had connections to Nazis – claims that turned out to be false - she told me: "I don't believe in guilt by association. I think if you live by that rule, you'll die by it".

Which is so true. The left often ends up eating their own, trying to maintain that absurd standard.

Even if their complaints against certain people were legitimate, de-platforming your enemies only serves to drive them underground. Letting people talk - even ridiculous people - allows everyone to openly critique and rebut bad ideas.

Germs fester in the dark, so it makes no sense to push voices we don't like into the darkness. Better to allow everyone to operate openly where they can be seen and held accountable.

As a proud Zionist Jew, I've copped my fair share of hate. And that's before the 'tolerant' left pretended to care about my ex-wife. That's just another pretext to attack me. But I don't think any of the people who attack me should be banned.

It should not be left to some shmuck sitting behind a computer screen in San Francisco to decide what speech is okay. If someone says something wrong, take it to the authorities. If it's illegal, then remove it. If it's defamatory, then courts can step in.

If I don't like someone, or something they say about me, I can block them.

Elon Musk's release of Twitter files (documents showing the FBI and other government bodies having a hand in the platform's moderation and banning policies) has exposed how partisan and corrupt that platform's moderation was before he took over. Imagine what the other platforms are like.

In the current environment, it's a mistake to rely on one social media platform because if you lose it, you lose everything. Speaking the truth in the 21st Century requires more than having a mouth, you have to use your brain in order to not be sidelined.

As I write this, I am involved in a major lawsuit against Facebook and Instagram's Australian fact-checkers.

I launched court action against RMIT University after its fact-checking unit wrongly branded as "false" my Rebel News report about a decision to cancel an LGBTQ lighting display at Melbourne's Shrine of Remembrance.

The CEO of The Shrine of Remembrance, Dean Lee, cancelled plans to light the sacred site in pride colours, citing "threats against his staff".

But without any tangible evidence presented by Lee and the media to back up these claims, I started digging around.

While interviewing sources at the Shrine, I captured on camera Victoria Police's protective services officer, who was in charge of security at the site, refuting the claims made by Lee.

"They're actually not threats. They're just hate mail," the top cop on the ground told me.

And then Victoria's Police Media team confirmed in writing that "police had not received a formal report" of any threats against Shrine staff.

I published both of those comments from two separate Victoria Police sources. One on camera, and one in writing.

Yet, RMIT marked my story as false, insisting, again without evidence, that "staff at the Shrine of Remembrance did receive threats to their safety which Victoria Police are investigating."

It's a bizarre thing for them to fact-check, even if it had been false.

Meta has teamed up with fact-checkers globally because they claim to be fighting disinformation that could lead to real-world harm, such as medical misinformation and election fraud.

Calling out a CEO of a war memorial for fabricating threats to justify his decision to backflip on desecrating the Shrine hardly seems to fit Meta's purported intent.

In their fact-check, RMIT wrote that "claims by far-right activists that the Shrine of Remembrance CEO fabricated safety threats against staff are unfounded".

Put aside their vain attempt to delegitimise my work by labelling me a far-right activist. RMIT's fact check marked my reports as false because they said I "didn't provide sound evidence".

Yet, nowhere in their 'fact check' did they print any 'sound evidence' of threats. Surely, that's the easiest thing to publish, disproving my story.

Meta's fact-checkers relied entirely on the word of Dean Lee, the man in question, and on the changing story of the Police Media unit.

A week after Rebel News published my on-the-ground reporting, the fact-checker was provided with comments from the Police Media unit that they were now investigating "correspondence" received by staff at the Shrine of Remembrance.

Since when does the media take the word of a CEO? Their job is to question everyone and everything and speak truth to power.

The implication is that if a CEO says something, even without evidence, we have to accept it as fact. If that is RMIT's idea of journalism, it explains a lot.

And to rely on a comment from the media unit, which had just one week earlier insisted that "police have not received a formal report", goes against every journalistic principle of cynicism and suspicion.

When Dean Lee made his claims, police said there were no formal reports. And even now, police only say they're investigating "correspondence", nothing about threats.

Meta's hugely influential platforms, Facebook and Instagram, slapped my articles with a "false information warning" and added restrictions to the shared pages.

Ironically, they deemed my report false because I 'didn't provide sound evidence'.

I'd shared the video of the man in charge of security saying there were no threats, and I quoted police media who said there were no formal police reports of threats at the time of publication.

I provided far more 'sound evidence' than Facebook and Instagram's Aussie 'fact-checkers' at RMIT Fact Lab.

It was once the case that you had to fight for the truth. Now you have to fight for even the right to tell the truth. And I've made that fight my life's mission.

CHAPTER SEVENTEEN

UNINVITED TO DAVOS

My journalistic career began by attending protests and questioning the activists. Some I agreed with, and others less so.

When Covid hit, my focus became showing the world what was happening to the once most liveable city in the world.

I'd report from protests and tell individual stories of people fighting back.

I met another independent journalist at one of the first lockdown protests. I immediately could tell he wasn't mainstream media, as he wasn't pretentious and rude.

Rukshan Fernando told me how he had a successful wedding photography business before the restrictions forced him to shut it down. Unable to pursue his chosen career, he decided to use his skills to show the world what was really happening in Melbourne.

The Sri Lankan wedding photographer had an impressive setup and was live streaming to a small audience. For now.

I didn't realise it then, but Rukshan would become one of the country's most critical voices throughout the Covid tyranny.

His style was simple. Hit the 'live' button and point the camera forward while calmly describing what he saw and how it felt.

It was something you couldn't get anywhere else—unedited, unfiltered, real-time footage of the craziest scenes Australia's second-largest city had ever seen.

Unlike me, Rukshan lived in town, so he was often first on site. As the protests grew in numbers and regularity, so did my friendship with this understated wedding photographer.

Rukshan is probably one of the bravest, most honest, and most loyal people I have met in this industry. His level-headedness in the heat of things and unwillingness to cower in the face of intimidation made me grow to love him as a brother.

So as soon as the borders opened and an opportunity arose to travel overseas to hold some of the world's worst people accountable, I asked my new friend if he'd come.

Without hesitation, Rukshan agreed to join me on a journalistic mission to the World Economic Forum (WEF) in Davos.

Rebel News was sending three others to join us.

We arrived in Switzerland a few days early to give us enough time to get our bearings and recover from the jetlag of flying from the other side of the globe.

We jumped in a taxi from the airport to the closest, cheapest hotel that crappy Aussie dollars could buy.

The hotel room was so small that it hardly contained the two single beds. There wasn't even enough floor space to open our suitcases. But we didn't care.

We just needed to sleep.

In the morning, Rukshan and I jumped on a tram outside our hotel and headed to the train station.

Rebel News had booked an Airbnb in a ski town near the Italian border. It was off-season, so we got a good deal. Or so we thought.

Usually, the WEF is held in the winter, but in 2022, they held the first meeting in the summer after Covid.

So the Airbnb was much cheaper than usual, but it came with many struggles.

After spending a few hours changing trains, we finally arrived in the small country town in the Swiss Alps.

We got off the train to see only a tiny wooden bench with a sign above it reading 'La Punt-Chamues-ch Station'. Gorgeous mountains surrounded the station, but there was not a person in sight, and we had no idea where to go.

I typed the Airbnb's address into Google maps, and we dutifully lugged our massive suitcases and backpacks - full of film equipment - in the direction my phone pointed.

We struggled downhill for ten minutes, barely able to carry all our luggage, before Google Maps crashed. Apparently, our trek was too much, even for the geeks in California.

After calling the Airbnb owner, it became evident we'd gone the wrong way. Without a taxi or uber for many miles, we were going to have to drag our gear back up the hill, past the station and all the way up a much larger hill.

With five days a week in the gym, I'm pretty fit, but it was a struggle. Suddenly those gorgeous mountains didn't look so appealing. Thankfully we had time, and we were in good spirits.

Puffed out and sweaty, we finally found our accommodation and, after dumping our bags, agreed that we both desperately needed food.

We walked back down the steep hill we had just climbed, down past the station and into the town centre, which was made up of a few little shops.

But there was a problem.

Remember how I told you we got a fantastic deal on the accommodation because it was off-peak? Well, that also meant there was nothing open except a tiny supermarket called Volg, and even its hours were restricted to only a few hours on certain days.

Oh, and there was one Italian restaurant open on selected days, but only ever for lunch.

We stocked up on eggs, milk and what I thought was chicken. Then we trekked back up the hill that was, by now, already becoming familiar.

We were exhausted. And just to top off a long day, it turned out that I don't cook turkey very well.

The next morning we woke early. It was a beautiful day. Summer in the Swiss Alps is more like a lovely winter's day in Melbourne. We enthusiastically headed down the hill to the train station.

Davos, here we come.

Riding the train through the mountains has to be one of the most breathtaking experiences in my life. The big windows seemed fake, as if the image you saw through them couldn't possibly be real. Mountains topped with a bit of snow as the sun lit up the trees on them.

I didn't know what to expect in Davos. We were concerned about potential security blocks as we had heard rumours of WEF police setting up checkpoints. But when our train pulled into Davos-Platz station, there were no obstructions, and we were free to enter the town.

As we exited the train station, there didn't seem to be much happening. There was no sense that this town was about to host some of the wealthiest and most influential people over the next few days.

It was anti-climactic after the effort to get there all the way from Melbourne, Australia.

We asked around for directions to the town centre, and were relieved to learn it only required us to walk up one hill. Tiny compared to the one where we were staying.

After about five minutes of climbing the hill, we made it to the Davos promenade, where signs of preparations for the big WEF event were everywhere.

The place was teeming with trucks, police, military, and organisers busy setting things up. The top of the hill landed us at the butt end of the promenade, a kilometre stretch of road where shop fronts, pop-ups and signage were being constructed.

We slowly made our way to the other side of the promenade, which housed the Davos Congress, where the main annual event is held.

It immediately became clear what a farce this entire institution was. Signs preaching climate change alarmism were everywhere, newly installed at a high cost for a five-day event.

Everything in sight was fake, and constructed solely for the enjoyment of wealthy globalists arriving in their private jets to set the agenda for the rest of the world.

The other thing that struck us was how entrenched the media were. They were constructing pop-up booths and advertising all along the street.

Obviously, the world's media were not in Davos to ask questions. They were there to network and, I guess, to take their orders. They were clearly participants in the entire charade.

Rukshan and I filmed an introduction behind the security barrier in front of congress before it was blocked. We then showed the world the enormous waste the planet's biggest hypocrites were willing to generate just to tell us what to do.

Back to the Airbnb, we went and waited for the rest of the Rebel team to arrive.

Over the next few days, to minimise costs, our team of five reporters decided to drive through the mountains into Davos rather than take the train. The trip took about 1.5 hours each way.

Police roadblocks had been set up, but in true Swiss style, the officers were incredibly polite. One policeman we met had lived half his life in Australia, and every day that we saw him, he was keen for us to stop and have a chat.

On our second last day in Davos, we told him how driving back the night before had taken three hours because of the fog. We couldn't see even one meter in front of us – it was the scariest drive of my life. The roads are barely one car wide with massive cliffs, and one wrong move would have ended us. Mind you, that didn't stop locals from flying through those mountains in their BMWs.

"Three hours? Where the hell are you staying?" he asked in shock.

"La Punt," I answered.

"That explains why you all look like shit. I couldn't even do that," he giggled.

"The altitude sickness hits too hard. You should be driving to the train, and it goes through the mountain," he explained, still laughing.

All of us had been feeling continually nauseous, but until that moment, none of us had realised why. Too bad we only had one day of driving left.

The train was great. It was designed to help motorists avoid driving over the mountains. You drove your car onto the carriage, and the train took you through the mountains. It changed the entire experience.

I wish we'd heard about it at the beginning of the week. Or at least, before the foggy night from hell.

Aside from the location of our Airbnb, the first trip to Davos was a massive success.

The most prominent decision-makers and global plotters all descended on this little town and walked the promenade as if they were untouchable.

Many were willing to engage with us because no journalist had gone there to confront them in the 50 years since the WEF had been founded. It was their safe space.

Watching their faces drop as they realised I wasn't bought and paid for - that we were there to ask the questions real people wanted answered - was incredibly satisfying, to say the least.

I got to confront a broad spectrum of powerful people, from the editor of The New York Times, to the president of Microsoft, a top Indian minister and the UN climate envoy.

My favourite interview from round one at Davos was definitely with the Special Envoy on Covid-19 for the World Health Organization, Dr David Nabarro.

Nabarro did his best to answer questions as he walked quickly through the promenade to the session at which he was due to speak. But the WHO envoy suddenly stopped walking when he realised I was there to hold his organisation responsible for their significant part in the Covid response.

"I'll stop now because you're asking quite aggressive questions," he said, with a change in attitude as bitter as a Swiss winter.

"And I didn't ask to be interviewed. This is an interview being done against my approval, and if it's used..."

I interrupted his threats by pointing out that mandatory vaccinations were conducted without many people's consent.

Even after threatening me, Nabarro continued to engage for almost ten minutes before turning to the camera and talking directly to our audience.

"I would like to say to those of you who are watching this, you know I'd be very happy to be interviewed normally about this, but to be ambushed..."

Well, I wasn't going to let that opportunity go. I quickly interrupted his rant and asked for his details, so we could continue the interview formally, as he seemed to prefer.

When Rukshan turned the camera off, Nabarro turned to him and said, "I hope you're proud of what you do".

It was a guilt trip. And it worked. We both felt a bit bad for him.

I held onto the interview, which didn't paint him or the WHO in a particularly good light, to give him a chance to honour his word. But imagine my shock when he never responded to my email.

The next day I bumped into Nuseir Yassin, aka Nas Daily. I asked the social media influencer and climate change alarmist how he justified flying to Davos to spread the WEF's message.

Nas got defensive and bizarrely responded by asking, "Do you eat meat?".

"But I'm not the one standing here pretending that I stand for all these things. You are," I replied.

And then, off he ran.

A week or so later, Nas uploaded his version of our interaction. He'd blurred my face, claiming he was protecting me from the backlash of his video—even though we'd uploaded the entire interaction days earlier.

Oh, and he edited out my final response. He cut his video at "Do you eat meat?" and then jumped to a monologue painting me as the hypocrite.

I couldn't believe he had the chutzpah to edit so brazenly. So in response, I took to the only platform where I have a larger following than him, Twitter, and challenged the global social media influencer to a debate.

I must have really annoyed him because he took the bait. His staff reached out to advise that if I travelled to his film studio in Dubai, he would agree to a debate.

No worries, but on condition that I bring my own cameraman in case the Nas team try their little editing trick again.

Nas surprisingly agreed.

I travelled to Dubai, and we debated for an hour in his studio before his girlfriend, who had never wanted the debate to happen, walked in and told us we needed to start the entire thing again.

"It's very messy," she insisted. "You're arguing with each other and not talking about the topics."

It was clear to everyone in the room that I had demolished Nas. I actually couldn't believe how easy he was to beat in an argument. I had expected a much tougher fight. There we were after flying across the globe, on his turf, with his entire team, and yet he barely managed a single coherent argument. Instead, Nas spent most of the hour hurling personal slurs at me. The worst part is they weren't even good insults.

I don't think either of us really wanted to film the whole thing again. And self-awareness is not his strong suit, so, I doubt he realised how badly he had been beaten. But we agreed to start over.

My cameraman was still rolling, filming everything, including the girlfriend making us start over.

The second round didn't play out any better for him, but the debate was done. We shook hands and laughed, and my cameraman and I headed home.

A few weeks later, Nas Daily's team uploaded an edited version of our debate. They cut the two hours into 26 minutes, using edits from both versions.

Even though their video was cut to make Nas look as good as possible, I still came out on top.

And that's not just me speaking. Ninety-nine per cent of the comments on his own video channel awarded me the win.

At first, they'd pinned the one comment they could find that said Nas had won the debate, but then they changed the pin to a neutral comment when the comment section began mocking their delusional attempt to declare Nas the winner.

In response to their version and attempt to declare Nas as the winner, I uploaded the entire unedited two-hour debate to a new dedicated URL (NasDebates.com). Which I couldn't believe was available.

Unaware that sharing the whole debate had sent Nas into a rage spiral, I planned to head back to Davos for the 2023 meeting.

I was excited to return to Davos, but my enthusiasm was tempered by a concern that security might have ramped up since our last visit. Heck, maybe they would try to stop me from entering Europe as New Zealand officials had done.

My fears were overblown, and we got into Davos without any drama.

This time my Rebel News boss Ezra Levant came along, and I ensured that on this trip, we didn't repeat any of the mistakes from 2022.

We certainly didn't repeat our Airbnb debacle, this time staying much closer to the action.

It was ski season, and our Airbnb was in the Davos-Klosters area. We also took advantage of the excellent public transport instead of spending each morning and evening driving up and down mountains.

Each morning we would head in early to the promenade and set up in a food court where there was a power point. One of us would stay, while the rest of the team would head out to find global elitists to interview.

To my surprise, security was basically the same as the previous year. On two occasions, police tried to assert their authority, but, both times, they backed down when Ezra put them in their place schooling them on press freedoms in Switzerland.

Swiss police are a different breed. First, they order you to stop filming, and if you push back, then they beg you to stop filming. They don't escalate like police in many places I've visited around the world.

The other fear I had coming into Davos this time was they'd change their approach to badges. The first time I visited Davos, everyone proudly displayed name tags as they walked the promenade. And the more important a person was, the more likely they were to wear a name tag. They wanted everyone to know how important they were. After all, what's the point of being an elitist if no one knows you're elite?

Badges were colour coded, and the ones we were looking for were white with a blue line. Those badges indicated that the wearer had been specifically invited to the Davos meeting.

It was impossible to recognise many of the people who attended. But as VIPs walked down the street, we would take note of the colour of their badge, and quickly Google them.

On this visit, a friend who managed to qualify for a media pass told me that guests had been instructed to conceal their name badges when outside of the secured area, or around the public promenade.

I'm guessing that was their big move to combat pesky little me.

But it turned out the important people believed it was more important that everyone knew how important they were than that they maintain their privacy.

Human vanity meant the "smartest people on the planet" foolishly gave us everything we needed. Again.

So thanks primarily to the unbounded egos of global elitists, our second Davos trip was an even greater success than the first.

Rebel News' most-viewed video of all time was our Davos confrontation with Pfizer CEO Albert Bourla.

The Pfizer boss had just left the secured area at Davos when my cameraman spotted him and his entourage. Ezra walked straight up to Albert Bourla.

"Mr Bourla can I ask you, when did you know the vaccines didn't stop transmission? And how long did you know that without saying it publicly?"

Ezra asked the question millions of people worldwide have wanted to be answered.

Now we had the man directly responsible right in front of us, with a microphone in his face and cameras rolling.

"Thank you very much," Bourla replied as he headed briskly down the promenade, picking up his pace.

"Why won't you answer that question?" Ezra continued.

"I mean, we now know that the vaccines didn't stop transmission. But why did you keep it secret?"

Bourla, with his head down, kept walking. But Ezra wasn't going to let him get away.

"You said it was 100% effective, then 90%, then 80%, then 70%, but we now know the vaccines do not stop transmission. Why did you keep that secret?"

"Have a nice day," a smug Bourla responded lamely.

If he thought that would be the end of it, he clearly did not know anything of Ezra's dogged determination.

"I won't have a nice day until I know the answer," Ezra shot back.

"Why did you keep it a secret that your vaccine did not stop transmission?"

Ezra kept going. Bourla was silent.

"Is it time to apologise to the world, sir, to give refunds to countries that poured all their money into your vaccines that didn't work, your ineffective vaccine?" I joined in.

"Are you not ashamed of what you did the last couple of years?" I asked.

Then Ezra fired: "Do you have any apologies to the public, sir?"

For five minutes, we were walking with and blasting questions at one of the most hated men on the planet. As a journalist, it was exhilarating. But more than that, it was vitally important work. We were asking questions that millions of people around the world wanted and deserved answers to.

While the ambush interview went viral, for me personally, it was just another learning curve.

It helped that there were two of us asking questions because thinking straight in the heat of the moment was challenging. Having a colleague ask something while you formulated the next question worked well. But while everyone was celebrating the footage, I watched back my performance and felt determined to do better next time.

In my defence, I didn't imagine having so much time with Pfizer's boss. Most interactions last just long enough to get in one to two questions. But Bourla was giving a talk on the other end of the promenade, so as it turned out, we had a long time to walk with him.

In hindsight, there were so many more thoughtful questions that I should have asked, even if he didn't answer. As good as the interaction was, it still felt to me like a missed opportunity.

Determined that just like our second trip to Davos had been better prepared, our third would be even better, including ensuring that my brain won't let me down in future pivotal moments.

The next day I was interviewing the Prime Minister of Luxembourg when a familiar childish bloke interrupted the discussion.

Suddenly, appearing from behind, Nas Daily pointing at me, asked the PM: "Sorry is he annoying you?"

Nas tried to take my microphone, telling the camera I was annoying and warning the Luxembourg PM to be careful of me.

To the prime minister's credit, he joined in the banter.

"I was a lawyer before if you need some help", he said to me before saying goodbye.

At that point, I didn't know Nas Daily hated me. I thought we had a friendly relationship and had been able to agree to disagree.

I followed Nas as he ran away, joking that he may need the PM lawyer's help for his role in promoting fraudster Sam Bankman-Fried to his followers.

But after rudely interrupting my interview with the Prime Minister, Nas refused to engage with me. Instead, he just said he had "saved that guy" from me as he ran back into the United Arab Emirates booth that had brought him to Davos this time.

He was clearly scared to engage with me because the last time we met in Davos, things had not gone well for him. And he had looked even worse when we met in Dubai.

But still, I didn't realise Nas loathed me until the final day of the Davos event when he thought he could challenge my boss.

"Aren't you guys fake news?" Nas taunted as he walked down the stairs of the CNBC booth with a camera pointed at Ezra.

"We're not bought and paid for like you, Nas," Ezra hilariously (and truthfully) responded.

Nas began to rant about Rebel News and specifically about me. In just five minutes, things escalated to the point where Nas was swearing at Ezra, "people like you are fucking dangerous to the world".

I must have completely broken the guy.

Do I regret it? Not even a little bit. Nas is one of the biggest hypocrites I know, selling his soul to the highest bidder. He wants to be a part of the evil WEF club in Davos who control the world.

Nas' greatest problem will always be Nas. He is a simple bloke. He's not a deep thinker.

I'm not even sure what his dumbest move was. Let's face it, there were a lot to choose from.

Was it his decision to edit our first interaction? Or was it agreeing to debate me for two hours?

Maybe his biggest mistake was making a fool of himself in front of the Luxembourg Prime Minister by interrupting our friendly interview and then running away like an absolute coward.

No. All of those things were dumb. But the dumbest thing he did was to try to argue with Ezra.

I'm fast on my feet. But Ezra? Ezra is next-level quick! So it was never going to end well for Nas.

But thank you, Nas, for all the content, helping me show the world your true colours and what we're up against in our fight to tell people the truth.

My favourite moment from Davos 2023 was interacting with the CNBC vice president. In fact, it was Joe Rogan's favourite moment as well. He recently featured the interaction on his world's number-one podcast.

Our UK reporter, Callum Smiles, had noticed a bloke wearing a VIP nametag outside the CNBC building. So, he casually walked past and googled the name.

When he realised it was the editor and vice president of CNBC, he raced over to let me know.

I casually strolled across to where the man was smoking while chatting with a woman.

"Hello sir," I said as I approached the couple. "Can I ask you what CNBC is doing here?"

"No," Patrick Allen answered abruptly.

As if that's ever stopped me before.

"I can't ask you?"

"No. I rather you didn't put a camera in my face," the vice president of a company that often sticks cameras in people's faces answered without even a trace of irony.

"Really? But you're here as an invited guest, and you're an editor for CNBC. Don't you think that's a bit of a conflict of interest?" I asked.

"I'd like you to go away. I haven't agreed to an interview with you. If you're doorstepping me, then go away," Allen demanded as he grabbed my microphone.

I warned him not to touch my equipment and kept going.

"You're meant to speak truth to power. Are you here to take your marching orders? Is that what you're here for?"

"Do you want to go away?" he repeated, clearly agitated.

"Not really. I'm here doing what you should be doing." I explained.

"Yeah? Please take this out of my mouth," Allen said, angrily grabbing my microphone again as he threatened to have CNBC's security team escort me off what was obviously public property.

It was bizarre. Patrick Allen, a man two to three times my size, was calling security because I was doing the very job that his company was supposed to be doing.

"What's the problem?" I asked him and the guard who was now standing beside him.

"You're my problem," Allen said. "You've been very rude to me this morning. You haven't asked me anything, so I'd like you to take the camera off me."

He illegally flicked his cigarette onto the ground.

"I've literally asked you questions politely, which should be your job," I replied.

By now, he was hastily retreating back into the "safety" of his temporary CNBC building.

But I was not done.

"I'm doing your job. I'm just not getting paid for by Klaus Schwab," I called out after him.

Another security guard walked out only to agree with me that there was no issue with my team filming on public property.

During our exchange, Rebel News UK reporter, Callum, entered the CNBC building to check it out.

He's a cheeky bastard like that.

Callum walked out with a massive grin on his face.

"You really pissed him off," he said.

"I was inside when he (Allen) stormed back in and told the staff that he wanted to beat you up. Or something like that."

Callum had forgotten I'd mic'ed him up earlier in the day because you can never grab too much audio. But I hadn't forgotten. We raced as fast as we could through the snow to where our equipment was set up on the other side of the promenade.

My heart was racing from the sudden exercise and excitement when we got to our table. The adrenaline dump was intense. Did we just catch the audio of CNBC's vice president threatening a journalist because I dared to politely ask him basic questions of public interest?

I plugged in Callum's microphone and brought the file up on the screen for Callum and me to listen to.

Boom! We got him!

The lapel mic caught CNBC's vice president and editor, Patrick Allen, saying of me to his staff, "I don't know. But this guy is going to get punched out taking pictures."

Allen turned out to be just another fool like Nas. Egotists who make it far too easy to demonstrate just how controlling and manipulative they really are.

On our first trip to Davos, we were pretty much the only independent journalists roaming the streets confronting these often unelected agenda-setters.

By the second trip, a few more journalists were walking around. They all said our actions the year before had inspired them.

I expect even more will be there next year.

What I am sure of is that the lessons I learnt and the experiences I had from the last two years will help ensure Rebel's on-the-ground reporting will be even better next time these Global Elites gather in Davos.

CHAPTER EIGHTEEN

THE HEART OF AUSTRALIA

Covering everything from leftist protests, Hong Kong protests, and Covid protests to personal Covid stories, election campaigns, and globalist gatherings in Davos has taught me a thing or two about journalism.

But early in 2023, I was going to get a new lesson.

Violent indigenous youth crime in Alice Springs began making headlines amid a raging debate about the merits of an Aboriginal Voice to Parliament that would be voted on in a national referendum.

While the spiralling crime rate in the remote central Australian town was concerning in itself, the story that caused the most outrage was brought to the country by our national broadcaster the ABC.

The ABC reported on a town hall meeting that had been called to address the city's crime crisis. Around 3000 people, almost 10 per cent of the Alice Springs population, attended the meeting in good faith, unaware they were about to be smeared as white supremacists by a national broadcaster that couldn't help but insert its inner-city identity politics into a local issue.

The fly-in-fly-out ABC reporter, who did not actually attend the meeting, produced a report alleging that the town hall meeting was a hotbed of racism, filled with white supremacists.

Locally and nationally, the outrage was palpable. I immediately knew I had to get there to tell the other side of the story.

"Rukshan, you happy to join me?" I asked my now-good friend, who'd previously mentioned the idea in a passing comment.

"Yes! Can you do next week as I have no weddings?" Rukshan enthusiastically replied.

Immediately my phone began buzzing as my wife, Rhonda, and Rukshan's wife, Rukshani (I find it so cute and funny that they share the same name), started trading messages in our private WhatsApp group.

Rukshani is the Avi of their relationship. Full of life and energy. Rukshan is a bit more like Rhonda, reserved and calm.

As you can imagine, our better halves were less than impressed by the idea of us going away again. Usually, our WhatsApp group is used by everyone to share funny memes created by haters, which we all love.

But when a plan like this comes up, our wives use the group to support us while simultaneously giving them a place for venting. Women are great at multi-tasking like that. It's a valuable tool for them, it's also been handy for Rukshan and me to have each other's back when dealing with our real bosses!

Alice Springs is quite literally the centre of Australia. Locals boast that their town is "closest to every beach" in the country, which I thought was a positive way to spin it.

However, getting there was far trickier than I had anticipated. There were minimal direct flights, and they were incredibly expensive.

I crunched the numbers and determined that travelling to Alice with Rukshan - and taking Daniel along for security - would cost Rebel News more than $6,000. And that didn't even take into account my salary.

I don't need permission for most story ideas, but with such a costly price tag, I had to pitch it to the Rebel News team meeting the following morning.

Needing to pay the equivalent of an international flight just to catch a domestic flight meant I had to explain to our team in Canada why the story was so important to Australians.

"I think this is the biggest story in Australia at the moment, and I feel it's made for Rebel News," I explained to the leadership team.

I told them how it was an opportunity to demonstrate the reality of our tagline, "telling the other side of the story", especially in light of the disgracefully biased ABC report.

"It's a lot of money," the boss began, "But you're our man on the ground. I trust your instincts, and I'm sure our loyal Aussie viewers will appreciate the work and help cover the costs."

With that, we were on our way.

As soon as we landed in Alice Springs, we began filming, and we didn't stop for days. The idea was to film as much as possible and then return to Melbourne, where we would produce and publish it.

I didn't know what to expect from Alice Springs. Watching television reports, it looked like a war zone, and I wondered why anyone would want to live there.

But when we arrived, I quickly saw what a great place it was. The town had clearly been neglected, but it was full of good people who were incredibly kind and hospitable.

The race issue – friction between black and white - wasn't really an issue for locals. People were just trying to live their best lives.

The problem of youth crime in Alice Springs affected Aboriginal people as much as white folk. Some of the solutions I was hearing from black fellas would be considered racist by the media if a white person were to suggest them.

There were ten things I learnt in Alice Springs that I was able to share with the rest of Australia:

1. Its remoteness means the town has never had a balanced voice in the media.

2. The loudest voices in indigenous affairs weren't speaking for Aboriginals living in remote communities.

3. Most Aboriginal people didn't know or care about the upcoming referendum.

4. Nor did they think changing Australia Day or the Australian flag would make any practical difference to their lives.

5. Aboriginal people were more concerned about the rise in often alcohol-fuelled domestic violence than about the virtue signalling that obsesses inner city activists.

6. Everyone, black and white, blamed the parents for the issues with their young people wreaking havoc on the town.

7. Police didn't have enough power to deal with the crime problem as the culprits were primarily too young to prosecute.

8. Community spirit was strong, no matter how the ABC portrayed them.

9. More money wasn't going to fix anything.

10. Organisations funded by taxpayers for decades needed to be held accountable.

Spending time in Alice Springs, all of these things became very clear to me. But sadly, I don't see much of it changing. Our country is led by moral grandstanders who care more about looking like they care than actually taking the steps to fix the issues that plague our indigenous people.

Even the Prime Minister, who famously jetted into Alice Springs at the height of the problem, spent only a fraction of our time on the ground. Neither he nor his Indigenous Affairs Minister bothered to get out and about in the town centre and talk to real people about the real problems.

It was confronting to realise that Alice Springs was not a safe place. We were forced to carry our gear with us twenty-four-seven so that nothing was stolen. And we were just visiting. Locals have legitimate reasons to be afraid.

At night, the town centre is a complete no-go-zone. Within an hour of our arrival, we experienced first-hand rocks being thrown at us, and that was even with the big, scary Daniel protecting us. It wasn't even that late at night.

The cycle of destruction of Alice Springs and so many other remote and indigenous towns and cities across our country will only ever shift when the narrative changes.

My one regret in Alice was that we were unable to stay longer. But like many of the lessons I've learnt from my previous journalism, I now know how I can improve on telling the other side of the story from similarly remote places across Australia.

I am determined to make it another mission of mine to be a part of the answer for Australia's indigenous people by changing the narrative so that people can see the truth, and in so doing, better provide real solutions.

CHAPTER NINETEEN

MYTHS, MISCONCEPTIONS AND ME

There are a lot of myths and misconceptions about me. I've been described as far-right, a Nazi (which always makes me laugh), an Islamophobe, a racist, a fascist, an extremist … the list goes on and on.

The only description they use to attack me that I agree with is Zionist, because it's not really an insult.

I am a proud Zionist, and those who use it as a slur usually don't know what it actually means.

The far-left and far-right are two sides of the same coin. They both hate me. And they both regularly label me a Zionist in an attempt to turn others against me.

At a lockdown protest in 2021, a hater walked past as I was conducting interviews and yelled from 10 or so metres away, "you Zionist shill, you Zionist prick Avi".

I'm not sure if he was far-left or far-right because lockdown protests attracted mostly regular folk and a minority of extremists from both sides. The media portrayed them as far-right, but the truth is that they were the most diverse protests I've ever seen.

There were even Islamic extremists at some of the lockdown protests, especially in Sydney, and they hate Zionists as well. But that's a whole different story.

So when this guy yelled out, I wanted to use it as an opportunity to challenge his views.

"Come, let's talk. Let's have a chat. I like people who don't like me," I called back as I began to head in his direction. Unlike the keyboard warriors who claim to fight hate, I do it in real life.

As I reached the man, ironically wearing a rainbow coloured t-shirt covered in peace and love symbols, I said: "Hey bro, let's talk about it. You wanna talk about Zionism?"

"No, I don't want to talk about it," the suddenly speechless man replied.

"What are you afraid of?" I asked the man who was now not-so-brave with a microphone in his face.

"I just don't wanna talk to ya."

"You don't want to talk to me. You just want to shout at me?" I asked.

"Yeah, I do because I don't like you," he stammered.

"Alright, so what's your problem with me?" I questioned.

"I think you're a Zionist, so I don't like you," he insisted.

"I *am* a Zionist," I answered proudly.

"Yeah, I know," he said, suddenly growing in confidence because he thought he had won the argument.

"Do you know what a Zionist is?" I asked.

"I think I do. But can you tell me what it is?" he said.

"Um.. you say you don't like me because I'm a Zionist. But you can't tell me what a Zionist is," I said, trying hard to suppress my laughter.

"Well, I think I know what it is. But what do you think it is?" he insisted.

I could barely contain my giggles by this point.

"I know what it is because I am [proudly] one," I answered. "You're only calling me one with a negative connotation because you don't know what it means."

He immediately declared the conversation "done"!

I turned to the camera and told the audience that these were the type of hate-filled morons the mainstream media picked off to make the rest of the crowd look bad.

For those of you who don't know, a Zionist is simply someone who believes in Israel's right to exist. A bit like a patriot of any western country. This is not the place to get into the thousands of years of Jewish history on the land or the fact that Jews, like any other people group, should have the right to self-determination, especially after what history has done to the tiniest minority in the world.

But for all of those reasons and more, I am a proud Zionist. And beyond that, it's personal for me. I believe in the preservation of everyone I love, including my mother, siblings and extended family, who all live in Israel.

I am an unapologetic Zionist, just as I am an unapologetic patriotic Australian.

When my detractors are pulled up on the fact they rely on character assassination instead of dealing with the arguments I am raising, they always answer, "Avi's not a real journalist anyway".

It's another great deflection.

I understand why people like to say that I'm not a real journalist. The established media don't want people like me in the press because I threaten to take away their audience.

The political class don't want people like me reporting the news because I'm effective. I'm not beholden to them for stories, and I'm not sucking up to them hoping to be invited on an overseas junket. I just try to get the other side of the story and broadcast the message as far and wide as possible.

The crazy lefty crowd don't like me because I'm pretty good at exposing their hypocrisy.

The irony is that we have a nationally broadcast daily current affairs show in Australia called 'The Project'. The show is mainly hosted by comedians, but no one gets upset that they are not 'real' journalists in the way that they get upset about me. The reason, I think, is pretty apparent. I'm saying the wrong things. That's why they don't like me.

Recently I was tailed over a few days by Tim Elliot from the Sydney Morning Herald for a long-form report he was writing.

I assumed the article was going to be a hit piece. In fact, I introduced Tim to everyone we met on those days as "This is Tim. He's writing a hit piece on me.."

So why did I agree to do it?

Probably a mix of a few reasons.

I've always been willing and open to talking to anyone. And, as I've already explained, I've never been afraid of attention.

But most importantly, I know how respected the Sydney Morning Herald (SMH) is to some of my biggest detractors. And specifically the "award-winning journalist" Tim Elliot and The Good Weekend magazine he was writing for.

The SMH describe The Good Weekend as "Longform journalism at its best. The definitive stories on the people, places and issues that matter to Australians."

So for them to publish a long-form article about me, by their own admission, means I matter to Australians. And I knew my haters would loathe that.

I wasn't particularly worried about what Tim was going to write. What could he say that hadn't been said before?

Well, as I had predicted, it was a hit piece.

Even so, I think it was a net gain for the reasons I have mentioned above, including how outraged leftists got by what they called a "puff piece".

Seriously, they called it a *puff* piece.

I wouldn't do it again, though. Not because it was so bad, it just wasn't worth the time and effort.

Tim simply republished old lies, which was what I had expected. He then used the time spent with me and my brother, Manny Waks, to create new ones.

The irony is that the award-winning journalist Tim Elliot doesn't have any formal journalistic credentials either. But again, my detractors don't care about his lack of credentials because he's saying what they want to hear.

On the last day that we were together, Tim took my brother Manny Waks, and me out for lunch at an Israeli restaurant in Caulfield.

Manny is a well-known international activist who does great work campaigning against child sexual abuse.

We were sitting at this Israeli restaurant where I assumed Tim wanted my brother Manny to spill the juicy beans about me. But Manny, with whom I don't politically align on many issues, told the reporter that most of the criticism thrown at me was unfair.

"Maybe the fairest critique is Avi's not a real journalist. He doesn't have the qualifications you'd have," Manny told the reporter.

"Actually, I find that complaint of your brother ridiculous," Tim replied.

"I don't have any qualifications myself, and I've been doing this for 35 years for one of the largest news organisations in the country," the multi-award-winning journalist added.

"Perfect," I laughed. "So if I don't like what you publish, I'll just tell everyone you're not a real journalist anyways!"

Tim, seeing the irony, laughed with me.

Many mainstream journalists don't have official qualifications, and that shouldn't matter. But it only seems to matter to my haters when it comes to me because, let's face it, it's just another way to discredit me and avoid dealing with the issues I'm reporting.

Tim didn't include that interaction in his article. Nor did he publish the majority of positive things my brother said. Instead, he ran with the only negative and absolutely subjective opinion from my big brother who, remember, has an entirely different worldview to mine.

"I think Avi doesn't care about many of the issues he rallies behind," my brother quipped at one point. And that was the quote that Tim highlighted.

That's how the publication this journalist worked for operates. The SMH regularly opens stories about me by calling me names (several of which I mentioned at the beginning of this chapter).

They introduce me as "Far-right activist Avi Yemini, who once called himself the world's proudest Jewish Nazi and was sued by his brother".

You see what they do there?

And when they want to go harder, they add, "he was convicted for assaulting his ex-wife".

It doesn't matter to them what's true or false, or what context is missing.

Manny did file proceedings against me years ago in the heat of a family dispute, but he later dropped the matter, and we're super close now. But they never publish anything beyond the suing. In fact, I'm close with all my sixteen siblings and both my parents, which you won't ever read in Tim's papers.

None of this bothers me too much. My reward is walking down the street and being acknowledged by regular people who thank me for saying out loud what they are privately thinking. Ordinary people thank me for giving voice to what they all talk about around the kitchen table at home.

Tim Elliot was shocked at how many people came up to me to say thanks and take photos as we walked together through Melbourne's CBD.

"I knew you were popular, Avi. I just didn't realise you were this popular," he said after the tenth person walked up to us in as many minutes.

"Mate, this is the real world," I told him. "It's not Twitter. People here love me and appreciate what I do. No one in the real world hides behind a mask, screaming profanities at me."

I think the key to my success has been to be myself. I don't take myself too seriously, and if people don't like my style, well, that's their problem rather than mine. I'm a larrikin for sure, but I think I'm a pretty effective larrikin.

But back to "award-winning journalist" Tim Elliot and his long-form article about me. This is how he conveyed the story I just told you about our walk through the Melbourne CBD ...

"By this time, people are recognising him. 'Onya Avi!' yells a passing motorist. A schoolboy stops to congratulate Yemini on his TikTok videos."

Now, I can see how my detractors would read that part of the SMH article and label it as a "puff piece." But imagine if Tim had actually published what happened and the details my brother expressed to him that he ignored because they didn't fit the narrative.

When haters are not calling me a "so-called journalist", they're calling me a racist or some other tag that I find equally amusing.

I've been surrounded by people from other cultures my entire life. I'm a Yemenite-Russian-Polish Jew who has grown up around Australians and who has served in the military under an Arab commander. My best mate is Maori, another good mate is Aboriginal, and my newest friend, Rukshan, is Sri Lankan. My most trusted cameraman, Benji, whom I take everywhere, is from Hong Kong. My first wife was half-Chinese, and I raised her Afro-Brazilian children. My now wife, Rhonda, is a blonde Australian with two Muslim kids.

I don't give a shit what race or religion people come from. I judge people based on their actions. And most of the people who call me hateful names are full of hate themselves. They have less "diversity" in their entire lives than I do in a single day.

I judge people on their actions and nothing else - not even their beliefs.

I mean, in my family, we've got views ranging from the far, far left of me to the far right.

I've got a gay sibling, and I've got heterosexual family. I've got religious family – a couple of my brothers are rabbis – and I've got anti-religious atheist family members. I love them all.

My family is a mixture of everything, but the best part is that we can sit down and talk whenever we are all together. Sure, it's loud, sometimes combative, and often it gets pretty argumentative, but at the end of the day, we love each other.

My closest brother (he's the closest at the moment, probably because we live in the same city) and I could not be more opposite in our political views. It's no secret that we have very different perspectives, but we couldn't be tighter. After a few drinks, we usually get into full-on debates and then our wives have to come in and referee. But it's all good. We're a loving family.

Our ideology is entirely different, but we manage to actually love each other. We not only get along, but we also enjoy each other's company. We can separate the person and the politics because that's what mature adults do.

I play by the same rules when it comes to people outside my family. I don't care what you believe in, but if we're going to talk about our beliefs, let's have a conversation with mutual respect.

You might think that my views are completely bananas, but you don't have to campaign to have me cancelled. You don't have to go into all sorts of name-calling or start bringing up things about my life that you have no idea about.

I'd say 90 per cent of people in the world would agree with that approach. But there will always be a small group of people who claim to be about tolerance and respect while actually being all about the exact opposite.

They don't want to debate ideas; they just want to impose their views on the world, and they won't hesitate to destroy anyone who gets in their way.

The really nasty people like to use my unjust minor conviction as evidence that I'm some sort of violent thug. That old chestnut is tiring.

People who say those things know nothing about my life. But from what they have observed about me, have they ever seen me lose my cool, let alone react violently to anyone, anywhere?

No.

Have they seen me lift a finger, even under extreme provocation?

No, of course not.

What they have seen is a larrikin who loves life and who mostly jokes around and laughs with people. But they heard one side of one story from years and years ago and they hang their hat on that to try to discredit me because they are too lazy or too cowardly to engage in a battle of ideas.

CHAPTER TWENTY

WHERE I'M MEANT TO BE

At the height of Covid, after being locked down for a year, I decided the time was right to lock in the best thing to ever happen to me.

I gathered my kids and Rhonda's - our boys (both 10 years old, my daughter 11 and hers 12).

"Guys, I'm going to propose to Rhonda, and I need your help," I told them.

Their faces all lit up, and they all yelled at once.

"Are you serious?"; "You're lying!"; "You better not be lying"; "OMG, so cool!"

They went through the five stages of handling serious information from me.

1. Disbelief
2. Looking around for a camera
3. Looking at each other, wondering if it's true
4. Realising it's for real
5. Getting really freak'n excited

If I had any doubt, their reactions proved to me that our families were right for each other.

The girls went on a secret mission with me to buy an engagement ring. I'm not sure where they got such expensive taste, but it was worth every last penny.

The boys came on a separate trip to buy four plain white t-shirts. When we got home, the girls distracted Rhonda while we wrote in thick black marker "WILL YOU MARRY ME?" - one word on each t-shirt.

My brother had invited us to lunch on Sunday, and he just happened to live around the corner from the coffee shop where Rhonda and I first met.

We weren't due at my brother's for a BBQ until 1pm, but we all jumped in the car early because I told Rhonda we should show the kids the cafe where we met.

She loved the idea, but she should have been suspicious when all the kids were so efficient at getting ready and in the car to leave.

They were so funny, asking "innocent" questions about our first date for the entire forty-minute drive.

We pulled up across the road from the little family-owned cafe in Caulfield. The kids were wearing the t-shirts we had made under their tops. An engagement ring box was bulging from my pocket.

Oh, and Winnie, our Covid dog, was with us because, well, how could we not include her. We were seated outside, joining two of the three tables they had.

The waiter came out and took our coffee orders – one half-strength latte and one strong latte with 3/4 milk.

Another red flag Rhonda missed was the lack of whining children demanding a milkshake or hot chocolate, and pastry.

With her oblivious to what was about to transpire, we waited for the coffee to arrive. I distracted Rhonda, who was facing me on the corner of the table. The kids had quietly moved behind her, quickly pulling off their tops.

They got in line, so the words were in order while I grabbed Rhonda's hand, pulled her to her feet and spun her around to see the message worn by our children.

Then I fell to one knee and pulled the ring from my pocket.

Even if she didn't want to marry me, she couldn't have let the kids down. Their face beamed with excitement.

Of course, thankfully, Rhonda said, "Yes!"

My brother's BBQ turned into a spontaneous celebration with a couple of siblings, their children and my father.

We announced our official engagement party for Sunday, May 30, 2021, where the rest of my family, Rhonda's, and our friends booked flights to celebrate with us.

But, Victoria was being led by a tyrant who called lockdowns at the drop of a hat. And two days before our party Daniel Andrews announced the fourth of six lockdowns.

We realised there was no point in booking another engagement party until the man-made 'State of Emergency' was declared over.

So I had to wait more than a year until Sunday, October 30, 2022, arrived – the best day of my life.

About a hundred people gathered at a pub in South Yarra - not far from where I'd run amock as a rebellious kid – for what they thought would finally be our engagement celebration.

It was, in fact, a noisy, crazy celebration.

Dressed in bright casual clothes with Kosher catering for my religious family and friends, it started as a lovely gathering of some of our most beloved inner circle.

However, Rhonda and I had different plans for the day that almost no one knew about.

We grabbed the kids an hour into the engagement party and went to a back room. We broke the news to them that we're actually about to get married.

Rhonda's daughter was the only one who knew, as we'd told her a week earlier.

The other three went through the five stages again, but this time much quicker as I hastily changed my clothes in the corner.

Now in a black suit, white shirt and tie, I was ready.

My daughter and son walked me back into the party to an unsuspecting crowd. The band began playing a slow Jewish wedding song as we made our way to the pre-planned position.

My brother Shneur who raised me as a little kid, now a progressive Jewish Rabbi, had agreed to marry us, so he was my only sibling to know of the wedding plan.

Shneur, grabbed three of my brothers, Yanki, who had just arrived in Melbourne from America for the engagement; Chaim, who came from Sydney; and Levi, who lives locally. He also grabbed Rhonda's brother-in-law Daniel and handed them one post each of the traditional wedding Chuppah.

They stretched the canopy above our heads as we waited for the bride to arrive.

Suddenly, the door opened to reveal Rhonda in a beautiful white dress, accompanied by her kids, one on each arm. My heart dropped, and the room went quiet.

It was perfect, better than we had planned.

The progressive Rabbi Shneur officiated a hybrid Jewish wedding for his right-wing brother and non-Jewish fiance.

I could see the tears flowing in the crowd as my big brother read the blessings.

And then, to finish it, I stomped on the glass.

"Mazal tov!!" the gathering shouted.

We were married. And as special as the formalities were, it was nothing compared to the kids' speeches.

The day before our wedding, I told each child they were to put something in writing, but they didn't have to read it out if they didn't want to. It had to be their words, with no input from us.

I'm so grateful they all chose to deliver them, and I can't do justice to how they read their speeches. They were the highlight of our wedding, and not just for me but for everyone who attended.

Rhonda's daughter, who's the oldest, is now fourteen. She improvised and added things off the cuff, like impersonating the way I walk, and mocking my overly proud Jewishness.

"I didn't put this in my speech because I took it out. But I kind of really want to mention this. Every time he watches a Jewish show or any show that has something Jewish in it, he goes, 'OH MY GOD, I KNOW WHAT THAT IS! OH MY GOD!' He thinks he's so special for knowing something."

Everyone roared with laughter. Her roasting was perfect, and displayed how playful, caring and loving our little family is.

The best I can do is let you read their speeches for yourself and, as you do, imagine the best delivery from the funniest bunch of kids you could ever meet ...

Rhonda's daughter, 14:

Hello everyone. I am writing this obviously in honour of the marriage of my mum and now stepdad, Avi. I remember the first day that I met Avi and it was on Australia day in 2019. The first thing I said about him was "mum why isn't he your boyfriend?" but, which was then followed by "mum why is he so short" which I think explains enough in itself. We spent a little bit of time with him and quickly got to know his very distinct traits and characteristics.

The next year, we met his two little terrors, **** and ****. But if I'm honest, it was not long before they were not just our mum's boyfriend's kids, but, our siblings. Although absolutely psychopathic, it feels like I've known them my whole life and I do look forward to seeing them when they are not around. I couldn't image my life without them in it today and in the

4 years we've known them, we have made so many memories, inside jokes and family sayings together and I'm so excited to make many more. I love them so much and wouldn't trade them for any actually normal siblings in the world.

**** [my son], when I first met you I thought you were a bit of a weird one but as I got to know you I realised what a kind, intelligent and absolutely hilarious person you are. You are the little man that I love to play board games with and you are always willing to sit by me while I do my maths homework so I can teach you a thing or two. You always have your own opinions and you are so interesting to talk to. Thanks for being my little spunky dude.

****[my daughter], before I met you I had always wanted a sister and the universe got me the best one of all. You don't understand how much I love you and how much you mean to me. I am so grateful that I have you to tell everything that's going on that I can't tell anyone else. We have gotten so close in the past couple of years and I am so grateful for all the memories and inside jokes we have made together. I love you so much and I'm so proud to call you my sister.

****[her brother], despite how much you call him daddy, you are not Avi's son but you are my brother, and I think you deserve a little mention. Even though you get on my nerves I will always look out for you. You are the one who has been through everything with me and it's good to know we understand each other.

****, **** and **** you guys are not just my family but some of my favourite people to be around. I love you guys more than you will ever understand.

Avi, it's your turn. Now, I make fun of you a lot. Let's just list a few things and, everyone, because he said he said he's gonna expose me at my wedding, this is me exposing him at his. He is the loudest person and anyone who has ever had a conversation with him about something he's passionate about, you would unfortunately know. Secondly, his extremely gassy manner and disgusting eating habits completely contradict to his alleged germaphobia because he's just weird like that. Also the way he walks look like he's trying be buff gym bro holding two extremely large bags in his arms and slowly waddling his way across the ground. If this seems mean don't worry, he makes fun of me too and he knows it. All bad parts aside, he is so kind and I am so happy that he is in my life. Every day he makes us laugh and he does so much for everyone. He is Definity the best source of entertainment and he even lets me steer the car sometimes, so, thanks for that Avi.

Finally, mum. After everything that has happened in our lives, there is no one I'd rather be here with than you and this family you have created for us. You are the rock in our family and without you, we would be ruined. Somehow you manage to look after 5 kids, yes including Avi and a dog and I honestly don't know how you manage to do it. I look up to you so much and admire everything about you. I aspire to be you when I become a woman and I am so happy for you on this amazing day. I can't express in words everything you do for me and I am so happy you have found someone that makes you the happiest you can be and I am so proud of you. I love you so much and thank you bringing me this amazing family.

Thanks everyone.

My daughter, 12:

I can't believe that it was only three years ago I met Rhonda, **** and **** because it feels like forever and now I think of them as my family and I don't know if I could love them more then I already do.

I am so happy that my dad found someone as amazing, kind and loving as Rhonda and now I'm not only getting a great step mum who I love with all my heart but also a little brother who can get on my nerves as much as I get on his but when he wants to be can be sweet and a great little brother and even though I hate to admit it I love him and the sister I always wanted and love so much she's someone I can share all my secrets to, who is someone I can trust and we might not be related but she is my sister.

And I am so proud to call them my family.

Rhonda's son, 11:

Hello everybody! Thank you for coming today.

Before Avi came mum was already full of stuff to do. But for some reason I will never know, mum adopted another kid called Avi.

But something we didn't know, is that 2 more came with him. It was like a package. Buy 1 and unfortunately pay the price for 2 more.

And related to them was a whole tribe, 16 more of them to be exact.

*But there were some perks like he was easy to scam. Me and **** [my son] abused that and he would convince mum not to be such a party pooper.*

But over all I'm proud to be accepted to this pack of a half sane family.

Thank you for coming and I hope you enjoy the party.

My son, 11:

Hello everybody! Thank you for coming.

Let me tell you a story about going from a Domino's eating monster to a gourmet food lover.

*There was a man named Avi known to some as Bobom. Bobom/Avi use to feed us this amazing food called Domino's. We once liked that food but after the first 10 pizzas it got old. But lucky for *** [my daughter] and I there was a saviour. A saviour so great they're not lazy to just feed us pizza for months. And guess who our saviour is? OF COURSE Rhonda.*

Rhonda has two somewhat normal kids and she also loves my dad Avi, at least I think so. But that's beside the point, the point is Rhonda doesn't just feed us Domino's and doesn't give in to buying us Nintendo Switches.

So thank you Rhonda for saving us."

CHAPTER TWENTY-ONE

COMING FULL CIRCLE

My mother often told me I was her favourite child growing up—a remark that massaged my ego over the years until I found out she'd apparently had many "favourite children".

Jewish people, we love the story of Joseph, the big-talking attention seeker in a family of 12 boys. He famously provokes his older brothers with his big mouth, and they throw him into the bottom of a well, where he is left for dead.

He survives but is sold to passing slave traders and taken to Egypt, where he works his ass off as a slave, only to be imprisoned for a crime he did not commit.

But then, in a remarkable series of events, 13 years after he was ripped from his home as a teenager, he goes from the prison to Pharaoh's palace, where his gifts and talents are employed to make a difference in the lives of citizens.

When he is reunited with his family as an adult, he tells them words to the effect that everything that had been intended to harm him actually worked out in his favour and brought him to where he was meant to be.

That story resonates with me.

I'm not claiming to be on par with Joseph by any means. Still, I am the loud-mouthed kid who pissed off his family, ended up in a pit of drug addiction and despair, served in a foreign land, was falsely convicted of a crime, worked like a slave running gyms when my heart wasn't in it and then - miraculously it seems to me sometimes - found myself running Rebel News here in Australia to hopefully make a positive difference in the lives of people.

My relationship with God is complicated – I'm not religious - but I do believe He's there. And looking back, I can say that all the difficulties He allowed me to go through only served to prepare me for what I'm doing today.

Being born into a large, boisterous, competitive family forced me to develop a big personality that has served me well in media.

Life on the streets taught me empathy for people and gave me huge appreciation for every good thing that I have, no matter how small.

The military taught me that you can't always be the rebel. Sometimes you need to toe the line and just get things done because people rely on you.

Running gyms developed my ability to market and promote myself. I didn't enjoy it. I would wake up every morning and think what the hell am I doing?

I'd be working from 6am until 9pm and hating it, then heading home to a toxic environment. But, looking back, it played an essential part in making me who I am today.

I never want to run for political office again, but that brief experience with the Australian Liberty Alliance gave me a taste of what it's like on the other side of the fence, which has been invaluable since so much of what I do now is reporting on politics.

In short, I feel like I'm finally where I'm meant to be and doing what I was born to do. I love my job, and I reckon I'm getting better at it.

I look back at some of the early videos I made, and I don't mind admitting I get embarrassed. It's good to look back and reflect on your previous work because it's a sign that you've grown. Just to be clear,

I'm not embarrassed about the views that I've expressed, even the ones I got wrong, but I do cringe when I remember how I've sometimes expressed them.

I bumped into a woman at a university recently that I interviewed a few years ago, and she told me: "You're way calmer than you used to be."

I went back and found the interview, and she was right. I was a lot more intense back then. So I'm learning and growing as a person.

I think Rhonda has a lot to do with that. As much as I learn by watching other people – the good and the bad – I think I probably learn as much, if not more, from Rhonda alone.

It's always good when she watches my videos because I can take note of the parts where she cringes and figure out what I need to change. It's always good to get brutally honest feedback from someone who loves you because you know they don't want you to fail. There's no doubt she is my greatest asset.

The other wonderful thing about my wife is that she doesn't care about politics. Believe it or not, that helps a lot. It means that when she gives her opinion, it's an insight into how most Aussies probably think. Let's face it, most people are not news junkies.

I may love attention, but I've tried never to do things just for shock value. I've also tried to be consistent rather than just saying whatever I think will be popular. There's certainly a temptation in the media to just say whatever the current thing is because you want to grow your followers and don't want to lose support.

The only time I've done a complete black flip was on Covid. During the first few weeks of the pandemic, I was really anxious about it. And, in truth, I think anyone who wasn't initially concerned was a bit crazy.

We'd never experienced anything like what happened, so we naturally trusted our political leaders and health experts. There was no reason not to. When you're being told that a virus could potentially kill you - and half the population with you - you do what you're told. And I certainly did, at least for the first month or so. I actually supported the first lockdown in Melbourne.

But, as time went on, and many things didn't add up, I started changing my view on how things were being handled. My point is that I changed my mind because the evidence changed, not because public opinion shifted.

My life has been hectic from the moment I came into the world. My relationship with Rhonda has brought calm, stability and a place of peace. She is by far the best decision of my life.

She has been my confidante, my encourager, my support and, quite literally, my lifesaver.

Her two children are exceptional, and the way Rhonda has loved my children has been more than I could ever have asked. (Not that they are hard to love, you understand!)

Our home is a bustling, busy whirl of activity characterised by laughter, joy and constant banter.

Rebel News is growing here in Australia, and I get to do what I love on the very same streets that were almost my demise.

I'm the happiest and most fulfilled I have ever been. And I am only just getting started ...

Manufactured by Amazon.ca
Bolton, ON

35087850R00129